MW01119096

1

Brigitta Dau

Crafting a Better Life

Creative aproaches to personal growth

Introduction

Hello. My name is Brigitta. And I am a crafter. I am also a certified life coach, certified pilates instructor, and...did I mention I'm a crafter? Yeah. Making things is one of my passions that lay dormant until around the time my father died.

Often, big events like losing a loved one, open us up to what we've been avoiding or putting off doing for the future. And we realize through these losses that our time here is indeed limited.

We are all here for a reason. Many reasons, in fact. 'There is something special in each and every one of us that we all yearn to express...and the world needs whatever that special something is.' I believe, that's not just a corny self help phrase. I believe it is the truth.

This is why I'm so passionate about life coaching and discovering what makes people truly come alive. One of the biggest highlights of working with people is when they overcome their fears and actually start living their lives fully illuminated...with passion and courage.

So, this book is a compilation of all that I know so far. I'm always learning more so I won't say that this is the end point. But, this book is full of helpful information that everyone can learn and grow from.

And...there are crafting lessons too! Every chapter begins with a craft for you to try. Even if you're not a "crafty" person, try a few of them anyway. Opening ourselves up to having some messy, unstructured fun is a great way to stimulate our individual creativity. And I'm a huge fan of having fun and making it easy to succeed! (much more on that in the following pages) So most of the crafts are quick and easy without requiring a ton of work or supplies.

The point is, whether it's making candles or writing a book, you have to be willing to try new things. And, taking fun, no pressure, creative actions is a great way to begin.

Actions.

That's an important word to mention.

Any exercises, suggestions, advice, including my own, is completely useless unless you actual DO it. You must DO THE WORK to see the results.

I repeat. None of what you read in this book will help you unless you actually DO the exercises...ACTUALLY DO THEM. Pondering their effectiveness leaves you sitting in contemplation...not creating lasting change. To make anything meaningful happen in your life, you must take actions towards achieving it. So, just reading this book isn't enough.

Whaaaaat? I know. You'll have to actually get off your ass and do some things. That's why I will recap each chapter with a review of exercises to try.

Oh, and one last thing...whatever you do, do it with joy. Regardless of who we are and what we're doing, we all have the capacity to add to the sum value of happiness on this planet.

"Don't ask yourself what the world needs. Ask yourself what makes you come alive...and then do it. Because what the world needs is people who have come alive" - Howard Thurman

Its time for you to create your life.

Chapter One

Jar of Wishes Craft

Whether it's the start of a new year, your birthday, or any day...this is a fun project that is a pretty reminder of the goals you have set.

You will need:

- pretty colored paper

- a pen

- scissors

- ribbon, lace, and/or fabric cut into ribbons

- a bell jar (or any glass jar you like)

- a doily or pretty fabric to cover the jar (optional)

- an elastic (if making a cover)

- ...And because I love glitter, have some glitter standing by!

Making your wish jar

1.   Cut the paper into as many pieces as you like. They should measure around 4'x8' but they don't have to be exact.

2.   Also cut one piece to be the label...it can be shaped like any label tag you like. (a circle, a heart, a rectangle, etc.)

3.   Write a wish on each piece of paper.

4.   Write on the label, "Wish Jar" or if you're doing this at New Year's, you can add the year.

5.   Cut a small hole at the top of your label and thread ribbon through it (approximately 12' or to the length you want)

6.   Roll up each paper and tie closed with your choice of ribbon, lace, etc.

7.   Once you have all your wishes rolled up, drop them one by one into the jar letting them fall as they may. (this is where I also pour a little glitter in as well)

8.   Cover your jar with a doily or pretty fabric cut big enough to flounce over the top but not too big to hide the pretty paper wishes inside the jar.

9.   Fasten with an elastic

10.   Cover elastic with ribbon or lace, etc.

11.   Tie the label to the jar.

TADA! You have an official jar of wishes.

And then, at the end of the year, you can open your jar and see which of your wishes did in fact come true.

Goal Setting

Why our ways of goal setting sucks, and why we will never achieve our sucky goals.

The most common times for goal setting is New Year's and Birthdays. Then, a few weeks go by and we notice we are not only off track, but we have already forgotten the goals we set.

That's because most of us set our goals ass backwards. We think of our goals as accomplishments rather than journeys. And because we don't ask ourselves why we want what we want, we easily give up at the first sign of challenge.

There is a golden rule of the universe, in my opinion...

> ***That which you desire has been deliberately put out of your reach so you can become the person who is worthy of receiving it.***

That requires a whole different outlook and entirely a new approach to goal setting. So let's begin.

Questions to ask yourself before you set your goals:

- How do you want to feel every day?

- Why is that important? Because everything you do, every goal you set, is to help you feel

a certain way. Obviously, we all want to feel
good. But my way of feeling good is different
from yours. For me, feeling good might
mean connecting to nature and my spiritual
practices. For you, feeling good might mean
the thrill of adventure. Or maybe, feeling
good for you is all about family and intimacy.

The clearer you are about how you want to feel, the clearer your
goals will be. AND, you'll have a clearer pathway to achieving them.

So, let's not wait. Pull out a piece of paper or your journal and ask
yourself some questions:

How do I want to feel every day? (Energetic? Generous? Grateful?
Sensual? Passionate? Creative? Joyful? Empowered? Sophisticated?
Inspired? Etc) Ask yourself this question at least 10 times and rattle
off whatever comes up.

And don't worry if you can only come up with a few feelings. Write
out what pops into your head even if you keep repeating the same
feelings. And don't get hung up on the words…I have 'creative
expression' as my top emotion and although that encompasses
many feelings, that phrase vibes for me so that's what I'm going
with.

After all is said and done, how do you REALLY want to feel every
day?

Now, on a different piece of paper jot down all your favorite
memories from the last few years. Feel free to include amazing
memories that go further back in time, maybe even your childhood.

Now look at all those times and ask yourself, how did those
experiences *feel*? Did you feel a sense of belonging, or excitement or
adventure or love? Don't over think it. Just write out all the feelings
that come up when you remember those highlights from the past.

Now go get a glass of water or take a few deep breaths. Because we're about to uncover your "Personal Signature Emotions".

Personal Signature Emotions: Who's really running the show?

(This exercise is based on a process created by Mastin Kip.)

Now go back and circle the feelings that feel the tastiest and the ones you repeated the most. (from both of the above exercises)

List the top 5 or 6 feelings.

Now let's do a little comparison.

For example, maybe your list of favorite emotions are:

- connection

- exhilaration

- supported

- grounded

- fluid/flow

Start with the first emotion and compare it to the next one.

What would you rather feel? Connection or exhilaration? Let's say you answer 'Connection'.

Move onto the next feeling for comparison.

What would you rather feel? Connection or supported? (These may seem similar but there IS a difference...you can feel supported without feeling connection and visa versa). Maybe you answer 'supported'. That means you favor feeling supported over connection. So now you compare the next feeling to your desire to feel supported.

Again, what would you rather feel? Supported or free?

Keep comparing until you can easily see that you have 2 top emotions that outrank them all...these are your 'personal signature emotions'.

How does this help with goal setting?

Your goals, while working towards them and ultimately achieving them, should flood you with the feelings of your 'personal signature emotions'.

Remember, the reason we set goals in the first place is to achieve a certain feeling. The more specific you can be in identifying how you want to feel, the more effective and relevant your goal list will be. You will also be more able to stick to and achieve your goals if you know "why" you want to achieve them.

And, how does knowing our 'personal signature emotions' help us create a plan to succeed?

...By creating opportunities to feel these emotions while going for your goals.

For example, maybe last year you set the goal to get to the gym 4 times a week. Well, no offense but, that's pretty boring and uninspiring and likely, you didn't get too far with that goal.

Ask yourself why you set that goal in the first place? If it's still on your wish list it's because you think it will help you feel better. But is "feeling better" a 'signature emotion?' Nope.

Let's say you specifically want to feel confident and energetic but currently, don't take great care of your health. Well, getting to the gym is a great goal for feeling confident and energized, while also improving your health.

How can you feel confident and energized *when* going to the gym? Playing certain music? Wearing specific workout clothes? (I had a client who had the most awesome colorful yoga pants ever... she said she wore bright colors to Pilates to inspire her because unless she felt inspired, she wouldn't go. Smart.) Is there a class or an instructor who you really enjoy? Can you watch your favorite show while working up a sweat on the elliptical? How can you feel confident and energized WHILE working out?

Again, what actions will help you achieve that feeling? Those actions and the feelings they generate, will help you stay committed to your goals.

The great thing about setting goals based on your most desired feelings, is that they will then have a much larger impact on your life as a whole. When you get your health in order, for example, you will have more energy and accomplish more every day. You will have better quality sleep and likely be happier. Just those few things alone will change your life.

I recommend writing your 'signature emotions' all over the place... on the fridge, your bathroom mirror, your vision board, (the next craft in this book) in the car, set reminders on your phone...keep reinforcing how you WANT to FEEL and follow it up with that question:

What actions do I have to take to feel that way?

Today, what will I do to feel the way I want to feel?

Less is More: Why setting only a few goals is better than a bunch.

What if this is the year that you write the book? How will your life change if this is the year you get out of debt? What impact will taking that trip of a lifetime have on you? What if you actually lost the weight and tripled your energy level? What if this is the year you get the dream job, book the gig, sell the script?

These goals are life changing goals. If you achieve these goals, you will be living life at a whole different level of the game. You will be taking risks, stretching, growing, and definitely dancing with uncertainty. Big goals usually require big effort and big risks.

Which is why, "less is more". We only have so many hours in a day and only so much energy to accomplish what we want to accomplish. That is why setting only a few goals will actually have a larger impact on your life than aiming for a bunch of little goals.

I usually only set one, maybe two big goals...for example, a few years ago I declared I would open my own shop on etsy. I did it and I'm still enjoying all that I get from being a part of that community. But that meant not only writing patterns for my designs, but also learning about seller's permits, setting up an on-line shop, getting press, advertising, etc. The list is long, let me tell you! It included me hiring people to help me with photography, web design, etc etc... you get the point. Massive action, tons of time. That year was also the year I set the goal of getting my mother's estate in order and creating a better system for paying her bills, handling her taxes, etc. That was a huge goal for me because I'm not skilled in finance. But I did it. I achieved both goals because they were the only big goals I set for myself that year.

Then, I usually like to set one or two small goals...like cleaning out my closet (EPIC!) But this goal is obviously not my priority. As joyful as having a perfectly organized closet might be for me, it's nowhere near as joyful as being an etsy shop owner, or no longer having a panic attack when handling my mother's estate.

And how you phrase your goals matters, as well. You want your goals to pull you FORWARD. You want to set your goals based on your future, not your past. For example, you are not losing 10 pounds because you are sick of feeling gross...you are losing 10 pounds so you can feel awesome in your clothes and buy a whole new wardrobe. The first example is reflecting on what is not working, whereas the latter creates images in the mind of something positive to move towards. And our visual minds follow whatever image we put in front of them...so, state your goals in terms of what you DO want.

What if you can't decide which 2 to go for? What if you are passionate about all of them?

How the Economic equation of 80% vs 20% can be applied to your entire life

According to time management guru 'Brian Tracy', (and economist 'Vilfredo Pareto', who was researching time management back in the late 1800s), 20% of your activities will account for 80% of your results. 20% of your customers will account for 80% of your sales. 20% of your products will account for 80% of your profit.

This means choosing your goals wisely, matters. If 20% of your actions create 80% of your achievements, then those actions are more valuable and more necessary to pinpoint in order to help you succeed.

But don't take my word for it. Let's look at some successful businesses we've all heard of...

Remember when McDonald's was 'super sizing' things? That was because they knew which items sold the most. Fries. I mean, come on, who doesn't want to super size those?!

And as much as they tried to introduce salads and healthier options, what still sold the most? Fries. Eventually the super size campaign went sour and backfired. So, moving forward, they did market research targeting millennials. Now their burgers are more "artesian" as are their billboards. But you will see they are also hardly promoting the healthier items. Their big money comes from burgers and fries. They focus on THOSE products because that is where they make the most profit.

The Gap also tried to expand into other fashions but lost money on all those fads. After firing their CEO, they came back to the products that earned them the most money...jeans, khakis, and t-shirts.

So, what are the highest valued goals you can set this year?

For example, let's say you're a writer and you want to write both a film and a web series. Which is the one that will bring you the biggest success? If it's the film, then focus on that goal and get that done before tackling the series.

You can further apply this principle to the daily actions you take towards your goal. (Here's a sneak peak but I'll go into this in more detail later in this book.)

For example, if you own a shop on etsy and decide this is the year you'll double your sales, you likely have a lot of work to do. You have to promote your art on social media. Therefore, taking beautiful pictures of your art is something important to do. But, you also may have other ways of promoting your shop such as buying ad space and utilizing various search engines. You may also want to offer a discount on certain items or run a contest on Instagram. So ask yourself, "When and how did I bring the most traffic to my shop?" Focus on the most successful strategies first and then if you get to the rest, fine. But you will have gotten your high valued actions done first.

For me and my shop? I found that getting featured in magazines was most effective and the cost was minimal. Yes, it required cold calling and yes, getting in front of editors was time consuming. But I sold more products from that approach then paying for ad space in the same magazines. So for me, press releases and shipping were high value actions. Instagram could wait.

When I asked my friend who owns a pilates studio how she got her clients, she told me *all* about the things she had tried. But ultimately, she narrowed her most successful campaigns down to 2 things: Yelp reviews and Google's ad words. All the other promotions were helpful, but those top two approaches were absolutely the most lucrative for her. So now, she doesn't waste time coming up with promotions. She goes straight to the actions that work the best. And if she's booked all day with clients, she doesn't have to worry about not having time to promote her business. She just has to make sure those two resources are up and running so she can carry on with her day.

Another example: if you want to lose weight you will have to exercise vigorously most days and alter your diet. We all know that. But, here's a little news flash for you...science has proven that although exercise is important, what you eat on a daily basis has a bigger impact on your weight and your health. So that means, making time to have healthy foods readily available is a high valued action. It holds higher value than carving out time to work out.

So, can you narrow your goals down to the highest valued goals? And will those goals help you to feel your 'personal signature emotions' on a daily basis?

...More importantly, will you love the journey?

Enjoying the Struggle...
Loving the lifestyle

Another reason many of us fail to find joy while achieving our goals, is because we don't actually sit down and decide if that journey is right for us. We get excited about achieving our dreams without questioning what it will take to achieve them, what our lives will look like if we do, and if we enjoy that kind of hard work.

The people who rise to the top of the corporate ladder, love the long hours and the pressure it takes to get there. The people who write novel after novel are people who love spending hours alone in front of the computer. If they love the lifestyle, sitting in front of the computer doesn't feel like work to them....

So, now that you've set your goals, ask yourself: "Will I enjoy the lifestyle? Not only on the way to success, but once I achieve it...will I enjoy the lifestyle?"

Back when I was getting certified for Pilates, my teacher asked all of us a very important question: "Do you want to be a Pilates instructor or a Pilates enthusiast?". Well, we were there to get certified so obviously we all wanted to be Pilates Instructors! He questioned us further... "what will your life look like? How often do you think you'll actually get to do Pilates?"

I can tell you the answer to that. For the past 15 years I have probably spent as much time in the car driving to studios, gyms, people's homes, etc as I have spent actually teaching. AND...aside from the classes I teach at the gym, I only manage to fit in a few Pilates exercises a day. In fact, there are plenty of videos on-line that are designed specifically for instructors because they only have 15 minutes to work out between clients! (whereas the enthusiasts, come take class with me at least 3 times a week!) And, I've also had to work with people in acute pain, debilitating injuries... and many with challenging personalities.

So, if I didn't like driving, I'd be miserable and probably fairly angry. If I wanted every day to be 9 - 5, structured, and secure, I'd be a nervous wreck. If I only wanted to work with super fit and easy going people, I couldn't make ends meet without another job.

The question then has to be, "Am I up for the challenges this lifestyle will afford me? "

If you want to be an actor, you will likely have to work as a waiter or caterer or drive for uber in order to keep your days free for auditions. You will also have to make enough money to be in class, hire a coach when needed, and do a lot of acting for free. (auditions) And when you do book a gig, you will then have to memorize lines, wake up for early call times, and deal with a multitude of egos. If you become famous then you will be stared at in public, be photographed without your knowing, and answer the same questions over and over at all the press junkets to promote your current project.

That will be your lifestyle.

If you want to run a nightclub, you have to like late nights, dealing with drunk people, loud music and flaky employees.

If you want to be in a band, you will have to practice for hours on your own, practice even more hours with the band, work nights and weekends, and lug your gear from gig to gig...at least in the beginning...

And, if you want to lose 100 pounds, you will have to change your lifestyle entirely starting with the food you eat. Are you willing to live that kind of life?

The fact is, you WILL face challenges. Obstacles WILL arise. So don't turn yourself into yet another obstacle by complaining about the path along the way. If you can't embrace the lifestyle (i.e. the challenges you will face) take a good look at that goal. Because yes, achieving it will likely feel awesome. BUT, with that achievement comes the work to get there. And if you can't enjoy the work, you won't put in the energy needed to actually succeed.

But, if you choose wisely, the obstacles, the struggles, the 'work'… won't feel like work at all. It will be just part of the journey.

But, are you ready?

> 'If there is something you really want, you are going to have to work really hard, take advantage of opportunity, make some mistakes, be patient, and above all never give up.' - Jane Goodall

And I would add to that, are you *prepared* for the life you say you want?

If your dreams actually came true, like right now…would you be ready for what your life would look like?

Who doesn't want to win power ball? Think of what those millions could get you. But what do you know about managing millions of dollars?

A lot of people wish they were famous. But, I suspect when the reality of fame came along, they wouldn't be prepared for the life fame brings.

Success comes to those who are *prepared*. Which often means a lot of hard work…for quite some time.

Ask any successful entrepreneur or artist if was easy getting to where they are today? I guarantee they will tell you it took a LOT of work. I mean a LOT of work. And now that they've 'made it', its even more work. But they will also say it is worth it, now that they are living their dream.

Let me share a personal story about working hard and succeeding in the end.

I'm originally from Canada and when I was in my 20's I was an actress working mostly in TV. I wanted to further my acting career by moving to the US. But, at the time, I had no working papers so even if I booked a job, I couldn't do it.

So, on one of my trips to LA I met with an attorney who told me exactly what I would need to do to get a green card. I did what she told me and eventually, yes, I got my green card! Unbeknownst to me though, I was actually following Jane Goodall's advice from the above quote.

Hard work?

I asked every PR person from every show I'd done, for a copy of all the press they had on their shows. That included international press from Europe, etc. (this was before the internet so that meant snail mail and photocopying, and a lot of long-distance phone calls) It took about six months of constant work to collect all the press I needed.

Whenever my friend (the Producer from a show I was on at the time in Canada) met with anyone from LA, I asked him if I could also meet with them or send them my acting reel...and convince them I was worthy of a letter of recommendation. I almost always walked away with a "yes". So, I was *looking for opportunities* to beef up my case for my attorney.

Mistakes?

Sure, I made mistakes. I ran out of money for a while (had to work as a janitor in a children's acting school) because I didn't calculate the exchange rate from Canadian to American money. I also didn't ask about other fees I would need to pay down the road as the approval process began. But, this mistake helped too because then when I DID move to LA, I could more easily calculate my real costs of living in the states. I was *preparing* for the life I was intending to live.

Patience?

Well, I was dealing with the government...which moves at the pace of molasses so yes, I had to wait a long time for my hearing.

And...*I didn't give up.*

In hindsight I'm amazed at how determined and absolutely ballsy I was! And I can cite many more times I've approached my goals with this same mindset...starting my own business, co-producing a movie, getting my Pilates certification, setting up my own etsy shop...etc, etc.

Anything worthwhile that I have accomplished has been through this same formula.

So in terms of achieving our desires, we have to ask ourselves if we are willing to put in the work it will require? Are we willing to risk making mistakes while creating opportunities? Are we in it for the long haul?

My year in retrospect

Do this exercise now and we'll use it again later when we talk about changing our behaviors...

You are going to write your year in retrospect. In other words, you're going to write out your year like it already happened and you achieved everything you wanted to achieve.

I like to start with "This was the year I _____". Include deadlines, like, "May 15th I put my house up for sale, and was in my new home by July 15th".

The clearer and more specific you are, the better.

Then, pull out your smart phone and put on the voice recorder. Record your year in retrospect...with your own voice. (And yes, getting used to our own voice can be barfy at first but stick with it and you'll get over that pretty fast.)

Again, do this NOW because you will use this recording later for another exercise. But for now, just record it and start listening to it during the day. (And save your written version for later)

Exercises to go back and review (and actually do!):

- Getting clear on how you want to feel

- Discover your Signature Emotions

- Less is more...only a few goals stated in the positive

- 80% vs 20%

- Are you willing to live the lifestyle?

- Are you Ready?

- Your year in retrospect

Chapter Two

Dream—Vision Board Craft

This is a creative way to bring your dreams out of your head and into a visual form.

<u>*You will need*</u>:

- 1 piece of poster board (any size you want)

- Pretty paper, scraps of fabric (for the back ground)

- Magazines, postcards, stickers (to cut out words and images)

- Crafting glue (Elmer's glue works just fine)

- Black or white acrylic pen (optional)

- Glitter...(optional but like I said, I use it whenever possible!)

Making your Vision Board:

1.   Decide what background you will want for your vision board. Consider mixing pretty paper with fabric to create a textured look.

2.   Cut the colors and designs you like and lay them out on the poster board to see if that's the back ground look you like. Once you're happy with your choices, glue them to the poster board. Allow to dry.

3.   Then, go through the magazines, postcards, etc to find images or phrases, or words for what you want for your future. Be specific and evocative. If you want to feel great in your clothes, choose words like "love my body" vs "healthy". Use words like, "I am one with the universe" vs "faith".

4.   Glue them all over your board making sure you can clearly see them. Feel free to write out these desires in your own hand writing with your acrylic pens. (Add glitter? Why not!)

Place your vision board where you will see it often!

Proven Strategies that Lead to Success

"The elevator to success is broken. You'll have to use the stairs...one step at a time"   - Jo Gerrard.

The Japanese have a name for the strategy that relies on tiny, continuing improvements to create change. It's called "Kaisen."

And with all the people I have worked with both as a coach and a pilates instructor, I have noticed that the people who take daily baby steps towards their goals have a better chance of actually achieving their goals. In fact most of the successful people I've met, don't kill themselves accomplishing tons every day. They take small bite sized actions consistently.

This might sound counter-intuitive. Most of us think jumping in with both feet means great big actions. But the truth is, rarely is anything in life 'one big action'. It's usually a string of small accomplishments that leads to the big accomplishment.

For example, let's consider running a marathon. Unless you're a top athlete, you will need to train for this goal. Having run one myself, I can tell you the training included *a lot* of short runs before the long runs.

Ask any writer how they wrote their book or script? They will likely tell you that they started with an outline and then plugged away at it daily.

In fact, look at yourself as a child learning anything...reading, piano, tennis...you weren't thrown onto the tennis court expecting to win a match! You likely practiced hitting balls off the wall, then volleyed with another person, etc.

I have another personal story about baby steps. Back in my early 20's, I knew I should join a gym. But I was totally freaked out about it because I'd never worked out in my life and was afraid I'd look like an idiot. Eventually, I said, enough is enough... 'you're going to chop this down into baby steps... one baby step a week!' (I don't recommend waiting a week for each step! Taking action every day is better. But, hey, I was 20...what did I know?!?)

> **Step one:** D*rive* over there and see what the parking situation is.

> **Step two:** *Park* the car and walk to the door, then go back to the car. (talk about a baby step!!!)

> **Step three:** *Open* the door and *ask* for information about the gym.

> **Step four:** *Go into the gym* and just look around.

> **Step five:** *Go to the gym and actually exercise.*

So, it took me about a month, and here's the irony with my plan. The gym was filled with gay men. I can assure you, they were not looking at ME!

And even more ironic, I now work in the health and fitness industry!

Baby steps literally changed my life.

Just to prove my point even further:

Dave Brailsford was the GM and Performance Director for Team Sky (Britain's professional cycling team). They had never won a Tour de France until Dave Brailsford took over and implemented his "aggregation of marginal gains" strategy (taking small actions every day). He figured if they followed this daily practice, they would win it in five years.

They won it in two.

And here's what it is: aim for improving 1% every day.

For example, think about your body weight. You don't lose or gain 50 lbs. over night. You make daily distinctions to either improve your health, or inhibit it. The weight is either gradually shed, or gained.

This is true for any goal you want to achieve.

But, when we are in a rut or frustrated with our current life, we want instant change and even faster results. However, to create lasting change and achieve big goals we have to break it down to doable, small steps. 1% is more than enough. Do the math...if you improve 1% a day...then at the end of the year you will have improved 365%!

Now for me, my 1% is based on a certain amount of time I work on a project. Again, I make it easy to succeed (I warned you, you'll hear that a lot in this book.) so I set the goal to work on my project 15 minutes a day. That's it. That's how this book got written. I sat and wrote with the intention of writing for only 15 minutes. Now obviously, if I went over and wrote for a few hours, that was great! But, if I had said I had to write at least an hour a day? I can assure you it would still be 'in progress' waiting to be completed. By working on it for only 15 minutes a day, I actually expanded the manuscript at least 1% a day.

So, where can you improve your life by 1% today?

Look at your goals, and decide today what a 1% improvement would look like. What can you do TODAY to get 1% closer to your goal? What baby steps, if taken consistently, will get you the results you want? Then tomorrow, ask yourself the same question. Every day, decide and do whatever that 1% improvement is.

How to Use Polarization to Create Clarity

You've heard it over and over: "Like energy attracts like energy"... in other words, if you focus on the negative than you are sure to experience more of it etc, etc.

Yes, that is true when you are visualizing an outcome or a goal. As I said in the previous chapter, focusing on the negative will only prompt your brain to create more of that negativity.

However, when it comes to making decisions, forming partnerships, launching projects, etc, having a clear look at what you *don't* want will point you very clearly and quickly in the direction of what you do want. Polarizing your plan is an excellent decision making tool.

For example, let's say you are producing a play. What don't you want? Likely, you don't want actors showing up late, co-producers who can't communicate, and flaky crew members leaving you having to do everything yourself.

Now spin it to the positive. What does 'what you don't want' really mean? For example, if you don't want to work with people who are chronically late, then maybe you want to work with professionals who do keep their agreements and actually have a track record of being on time. When assembling your production staff you will also be looking for people who are good communicators and who again, have some experience so you know they can follow through. And to ensure you're not left holding the bag maybe means, you want a more collaborative team so its easier to delegate. Do you see how flipping the negative to the positive gives you a clear roadmap as to who you will work with?

You can use this for all of your decisions.

Let's say you are wanting to take a yoga class. Being clear will help you choose the right class. Personally, I don't want to leave class feeling sore, overheated, and needing a nap! So then how *do* I want to feel? Connected to my body in a positive way and more energized than I was before class? Sounds good to me! Having that clarity will help you choose the time, the instructor, and type of class you're going to take.

And, when you make the big decisions...buying a house, starting a new business, creating a project involving multiple partners...you can use this clarity tool to ensure you are gathering the right people to help you see your vision come true. This also helps you spot the red flags...that good ol' 'gut feeling' you have about certain people. Likely they are exhibiting something from your "don't want" list.

"Start the way you want to finish" is not just an old saying, It is absolutely true when starting something big. Choose your team wisely...by knowing what you want and what you don't want.

Breaking Bad Habits and Making New Good Habits

It ain't easy, that's for sure. It's Hard with a capital H. We humans despise change even if we know what we are doing is bad for us. We prefer to repeat our behavior rather than go through the work it takes to change it.

But, we know that change is possible. If you can learn bad habits, you can learn good ones too. Right? Absolutely.

First, it helps to understand our brains and why we are literally creatures of habit.

We are built to conserve energy. Back in the Neanderthal days, it took a good deal of effort to hunt down our dinner. As a result, we got really good at remembering where and how we had the most success with the most amount of ease. Finding high calorie, high fat food with the least amount of effort was ideal and necessary for our survival. So getting food in that fashion became habitual. So did everything else...because learning anything new takes energy. And we needed to conserve our energy for our survival.

And if whatever action you're taking ends in a positive result? (ie tastes good, feels good, etc) You are more likely to create a habit based on that behavior...even if you know what you're doing is bad for you. (Smoking is a great example...)

Habits have 3 components to them: the trigger, the behavior, and the reward. Once the reward bell is sounded, the brain looks for ways to repeat that pattern.

Let's use cheesecake as an example. What happens first? You see the cake (trigger), then you eat the cake (behavior), it tastes friggin' awesome!!! (reward). And because our brains still have primal reactions when it comes to food, the fact that cheesecake is clearly high in calories, fat, and sugar is also triggering our brain. Without our even knowing, our brain is saying, "Remember where you found this food...and repeat this pattern." Ah...and a habit it formed. See cake, eat cake, yummy cake, repeat.

We start creating habits the second we are born. We taste that breast milk and know exactly where to find it again...it tastes great and is high in calories and nutrients. 'Remember where I found this and repeat this pattern'. This is how we survive.

So even bad behaviors, if they originally felt good to us, and if they are repeated a few times, will become habits.

Also, you may reach for that habit when you're stressed out or having a bad day. Going back to the cheesecake example, lets say you just got in a huge fight with your boss. You're upset and "craving" cheesecake. Why cheesecake? Why now? Because your brain is remembering a habit that results in you feeling GOOD. That's why "comfort food" is what it's called...you feel good eating those foods from previous experiences that have now become a habitual way of lifting your moods. (And food manufacturers take major advantage of this. That's a whole other book!!!)

However, yes, we can break those bad habits and create good new ones. Absolutely.

But before we get into that, I'd like call Bullshit on something our society seems to revere as the highest ranking value: Willpower.

If you think you don't have enough willpower, let me remind you that at some point, you stood. And then you walked...and eventually ran. Did you fall down? Yup, you did. You fell many, many times. Did you still keep at it until you could walk and run without falling? Yes you did. So we all have willpower. Let's put that excuse to rest.

Breaking bad habits and creating new healthy ones isn't about willpower.

Willingness vs Willpower

Ask anyone who has ever made a big change in their life: quit smoking, changed careers, left a bad relationship, finished their manuscript...willpower had little to do with how they followed through. What they *did* have was a very strong desire to change (failure was not an option), and the *willingness* to feel uncomfortable when the going got tough. They also had a plan. Not just the action steps required to achieve their goal, they also had a plan for how to handle the obstacles that would likely come up. That's where willingness is crucial for creating lasting change.

Let's use quitting smoking as an example (which I did myself 30 years ago). Why do you want to quit? Don't use your spouse's concerns or your children's guilt trips as reasons why, unless they resonate for you. Why do YOU want to quit smoking (...fill in the blank for anything you want to change). Get very clear and excited about seeing yourself as the person you want to become. Visualize it and fully engage all of your senses. When you have already overcome the challenge, how will that feel? How will your life look? What will you say and hear other's saying? How will your body feel? Again, really connect with your feelings.

Now ask yourself, what you're going to have to give up to achieve this goal. What are some of the "negatives" about changing this behavior? Lasting change means sacrificing some things. Take the time now to acknowledge what losses you will have to accept.

Ambivalence is a normal part of goal setting that most of us confuse with a signal to give up. Again, our resistance to change is huge. But, until your new behavior is habitual, it will take a lot of energy and probably some trial and error before it starts to feel easy.

Let's go back to my example of quitting smoking. There is a lot to give up when you quit smoking. For example, aside from the addiction itself, smokers often have to give up some social situations. When I quit, I avoided seeing my smoking friends for a few weeks. I avoided the smoke filled bars (you were allowed to smoke inside bars back then...and on planes!) At parties, I stayed inside while my smoking friends went outside. That was a big sacrifice for me because I had close ties with those people...we spent hours out in the cold smoking and gossiping. (And seriously, it was cold...I'm from Canada, remember!) There was some loneliness and serious boredom for me to overcome. Was it still worth it to me to quit? Was I willing to stay inside and make new connections with the non-smokers? Yes, I was *willing*. I wanted to have the label: "non-smoker" be my new identity.

Honor your ambivalence. Allow room for yourself to feel the crummy stuff. But don't let it take charge. Instead, write it out. (Do **not** do this in your head.) Write out all the reasons you don't want to go for it and include the things you will have to give up. And then for each item on your list, decide... "am I willing to feel and experience this in order to achieve my goal?"

If you truly want to change and know why, you will be able to answer this question with an earnest "yes". But, let's not be naive either. This is an opportunity for you to be honest with your limitations and prepare for them in advance. And every time they come up, you can remind yourself to revisit WHY you want it and that you are WILLING to handle this present challenge.

A lot of people post "Am I willing?" all over their home and office as reminders. Some people set reminders on their phone so when they enter into a *"potential ambivalence challenge"*, they are prepared to take action. And some people enlist their friends to remind them of why they want to change and how great they will feel when they've achieved it.

Whatever works best for you, do it! Again:

- WHY do you want to make this change?

- WHAT obstacles might come up and WHAT

will you have to give up?

- Write it out!

Are you WILLING to feel the feelings that will inevitably come up should these obstacles actually happen? (Go through each item on your list.)

UFO's

"UFO" is a term a crafters use to name "Unfinished Objects".

Creative people are notorious for enthusiastically starting projects, but then lacking the discipline and focus to finish them through to the end.

Here's the good and bad news: The ability to follow through is a habit, not an inherent skill or talent.

Again, habits are learned behaviors (be they good or bad), that have been repeated consistently. After regular, consistent repetition, those behaviors become habitual. So finishing your projects is something you have to train yourself to do.

Step one:

Define Completion. What will it look like for you to finish the project? Maybe finishing your acting or voice over reel defines completion for your goal. Maybe getting all your receipts to your financial advisor by a specific date means completion for you. Perhaps getting your resume perfectly ready for submission is the project you are avoiding completion on.

Define what it will look like when you have achieved completion.

Step two:

Work it backwards. Plot the steps to get this project done...
backwards. What was the last step you took before completion?
What was the step before that? etc. Going backwards helps
us overcome overwhelm because we are not used to plotting
backwards when goal setting. Normally we start at the beginning
and can only see the monumental work ahead of us. Planning in
reverse interrupts that thought process so we can more easily list
the steps required.

Step three:

Know thyself! When are you most effective? We are all "in the
zone" at different times of the day. Morning people are not effective
in the evening and visa versa. Forget what you've been told about
work hours and ask yourself "When am I most effective? When do I
have the most energy and passion?" Then, schedule those hours to
work on your goal.

(I recommend actually scheduling this into your calendar and
setting reminders if necessary.)

If your peak time isn't an option (maybe you work full time or
have the kids during that time), then see if there is a small change
you can make to your schedule to allow for another potential peak
time to open up. Maybe trading a morning workout for an evening
one will open up more quiet time. Maybe not checking Facebook
until the evening will create more time that you are presently
squandering during your lunch breaks. Or maybe, NOT checking
Facebook in the evening will help you get to bed earlier thus helping
you have more energy in the morning.

Getting creative and carving out other peak times will still help you create the habit of completion. And, you will be more naturally drawn to doing the work because your energy will be on your side.

Remember, small, regular, consistent steps create huge change and success over the long run.

<u>Things to go back and Review:</u>

- Baby Steps or 1% a day

- Polarize for Clarity

- Review how habits are formed

- Willingness vs Willpower

- UFO's

Chapter Three

Flower Filled Ice Cubes Craft

Whether it is a bridal shower, a fun afternoon with girlfriends, or Valentine's Day with your lover, these colorful ice cubes at so much fun for very little cost or time. (And guys, make these for your girlfriends and see how much they appreciate you!)

You will need:

- An ice-cube tray

- A freezer

- Edible flowers

- Water (ideally filtered)

- A fork

Making your ice cubes:

1.   Thoroughly wash the edible flowers first. Then, rip them into smaller pieces and put them in your tray. Vary the colors throughout the tray.

2.   Add filtered water.

3.   The flowers may float to the top so use a fork to push them back down into the center of the cube. (They may still float up again, but don't worry...they will still look lovely.)

4.   Place in the freezer until frozen completely.

Enjoy your beautiful, colorful ice cubes!

Self-Sabotage

Why we do it and how to catch ourselves before doing it again.

First of all, let's collectively take a deep breath and sigh it out with a bucket load of self-forgiveness. Absolutely everybody on the planet has sabotaged their own happiness at some point in their lives. Some do it in public, in sports, or politics. Some do it privately in their relationships or with their work.

Regardless of your fame, wealth, health, religion...at some point you will find yourself getting in your own way despite your best efforts. And self sabotage is always, always, ALWAYS about fear.

Some people need to know *why* they sabotage themselves so let's go over that first. Having said that, knowing the *why* isn't necessary to create change. So, if you can't figure out why you stop yourself, don't worry. It's more important to recognize *how* you stop yourself.

But first, for those of you who like to psychoanalyze themselves (I'm one of those people!) let's get into the *why's*.

Fear of being Secretly, Fundamentally Flawed

For some of us, we have a belief from childhood that we are unworthy of success because something is secretly wrong with us and gaining success would expose our hidden flaw.

Which, if you think about it, this is a good reason to block your success. If you believed that there was something fundamentally wrong with you, why on earth would you put yourself out there for a loving relationship, awesome job, or full creative expression.

Fear of Outshining and Losing the People we Love

Some people experienced this in their childhood. Maybe they got an "A" on a test and their friend decided not to talk to them anymore. As an adult we can see that is clearly an act of envy but to a child, it simply means loss, abandonment, and pain.

And many well meaning parents instilled this belief in their children to keep their less scholastically talented sibling safe from having their feelings hurt. "That's great that you got an 'A...' but let's not put it on the fridge because Bobby hasn't gotten an 'A' yet." Again, well meaning, but creating the belief: "Don't outshine people. It will hurt their feelings."

Fear of Too Much Work

We know that more success often brings more work. But this belief is not about being busy. This fear is about being overwhelmed and inundated with work that is horribly unpleasant and exhausting. Again, look back at your past and see if you were ever overwhelmed with work to achieve your good grades, your spot on the team, etc.

If the work felt tedious and pressure based, you likely view success as a burdensome experience and let's face it...nobody liked doing heaps of homework.

Fear of not being allowed to Fail...the Golden Child

This is a less common reason, but I've had several clients with this belief. Some people were raised by a family that was unrealistically positive. Their thought process was that if they raised their children to believe they can do no wrong, they'd be more confident, self-assured, etc. But the problem is, for the child they're only getting the message that they are perfect. So, what does that mean if they don't get accepted to their college of choice? They aren't supposed to fail...they are perfect, remember?

This funky belief stops many people before they even start. It creates a hell of a lot of fear and pressure for someone who wants to take a risk or try something new...

Fear of Joy

As bizarre as that sounds, this is incredibly common. Yet I've rarely heard it discussed by experts and even then, only heard about it when dealing with eating disorders, addiction, and abuse. But, I see it with many of my clients who don't have addictions or abuse in their past. So, I'm going to go into more detail with this.

On its face, this sounds ludicrous. Who doesn't want to be happy? Of course that's what everybody wants. However, some of us have negative past experiences when we felt joyful. For example, sometimes marriages end when children are quite young. Chances are, their kid's lives were pretty happy until the family broke up. But the trauma of having their family pulled apart can be earth-shattering for children. Children don't have the reasoning capacity that adults do and often will think they are responsible for the family's destruction. We've all heard that before...children thinking their parents split up because of something they personally did wrong. And so their joy was quickly turned into pain and a new belief was created.

And let's not underestimate the power of envy. This is another example of associating negative feelings to joy. Often when a person starts succeeding at their goals, an envious friend or family member will make a remark that hurts their feelings. Sometimes that envious person will go so far as to take actions against them like buying them a box of chocolates when they know sugar is a trigger for that person. Whether it's a mean comment or a destructive action, the feeling inflicted is the same...pain.

So, in this case, what does this have to do with why we sabotage ourselves when we are feeling good?

Because if you associate feeling good with a punishment on the horizon, you are more likely to create something painful *now* rather than wait to get hit by something unknown. It's a way of having control over your pain, as dysfunctional as that may sound. One of my clients described it as "I'm cutting myself off at the knees before someone else does".

Think back to a time when things were going great and then you did something to sabotage it. Maybe you lost a few pounds and "treated" yourself to a slice of pizza that turned into a week long binge. Maybe you got a promotion and that night you celebrated a little too hard and ended up with a DUI. Maybe you had an amazing weekend away with your spouse and then picked a fight on the drive home.

I distinctly remember leaving a yoga class feeling absolutely fantastic. The sun was shining, I felt great in my skin, and then the thought, "Muffins" popped into my head. Really?!? That would have been the perfect behavior to sabotage my bliss...loading up on carbs and sugar.

At the time this happened, I was working with a life coach and told her how confused I was about this reaction: One-second feeling great, and then wanting to ruin it as quickly as possible. Together we realized that for me, anytime I have lost weight, gotten healthy, or taken any major step towards my own health, I've binged. We traced this back further to how things were in my family growing up. The pattern was evident. I would accomplish something, I'd be rewarded with minimal praise, and then the expectations were raised and I was given a new challenge to face. Meaning, anytime I did well, I'd have to do better the next time. So feeling good about what I had accomplished was quickly followed with the pressure to do better. It became clear that I associated feeling good with feeling pressure. And rather than not knowing when that pressure might come up, I preferred to just kill the joy as quickly as possible and get it over with.

So again, it's about fear and control.

Does this resonate for you? If it does, take a few minutes and journal about your childhood. *Do this now before reading on.* See if you can figure out what patterns were created around joy, and what pain you experienced that you attributed to feeling good. What patterns stem from those experiences? The clearer you can be, the better.

Then when you are tempted to sabotage, you can be clear about what is really going on. You can even ask yourself... "I notice I'm resisting feeling good...what are my beliefs about that? What bad thing am I thinking might happen, if I allow this joy into my life?"

Being curious about your feelings around joy is an invaluable resource if this is your issue. Because whatever your behavior is, it's unique to you and your history.

These are the most common reasons for sabotaging ourselves. You likely don't have all of these issues but maybe have one or two. Or maybe none. Maybe you have other awesome excuses as to why you can't get out of your own way. Welcome to the human race.

Discerning how we fuck ourselves up...and what to do about it

Procrastination

We all procrastinate sometimes. After all, work is called "work", not "play". But, some of us are sabotaging our dreams by letting procrastination run amuck. If you are procrastinating on something you are passionate about... writing a script, creating a support group, building a website... then you already know, you are indeed sabotaging yourself. (And, let me add, of all the hundreds of people I've worked with, only ONE does well under the pressure of procrastination. ONE!!! And I'm betting you aren't number two!)

So, if you're procrastinating, ask yourself this... "What am I more committed to?" For example, are you more committed to watching Netflix than writing your spec script?" "Are you more committed to 'happy hour' than saving your money to get out of credit card debt?" Are you more committed to sleeping in than getting up 1/2 hour early to go for a jog? I can assure you, if your house was on fire you would not be committed to remaining in bed. So, why are you so committed to staying comfortable when it comes to your goals?

Obviously, you are afraid of something. So, let's figure that out. Ask yourself...

"If the worst case scenario were to happen, what would that mean to me?" and follow that up with, "and then what would happen?"

For example, I had a client who was concerned about starting a new business. From personal experience, I will tell you that starting any new venture is time consuming and offers no guarantees. This is why many people are happy managing a Peet's coffee vs opening their own coffee shop. Going your own way takes money, courage, and a shit-load of energy.

So, he had reasons to be nervous. But he'd done the research, had a good financial plan, and for all intents and purposes, it looked like a risk that would be worth taking.

So I asked, "If the worst case scenario were to happen, what would that mean to you?"

He said he'd lose a substantial amount of money.

"And then what would happen?" I asked

"I might have to move, I might have to get another job, I'd be pretty broke."

"And then what would happen?"

"Take out a loan...if I could..."

"And if you couldn't take out a loan, then what?"

"I guess I'd have to ask my father to help me out"

"And then what?

"He'd see that he was right. I'm terrible at business and should have just followed in his footsteps instead."

"And then?"

"He'd think I'm an embarrassment to the family."

BINGO!!!!

He was procrastinating because he believed that if he failed, his father would be ashamed of him. Now THAT is a very scary thought for most of us. As much as we know we are "grown-ups," we still don't want to let our parents down. And nobody wants to feel like a cause for family shame or have their weaknesses exposed for the world to see.

No wonder he was avoiding going for it fully. His identity and self esteem were at stake. He was *more committed* to keeping his self esteem intact and not upsetting his father. After realizing that, he could then acknowledge to himself that he was being irrational and acting out of childhood fears.

From that point onward, he could look his procrastination in the eye and override it.

So, the question is, what are you more committed to than going for your dreams? And more importantly, why? What is the worst case scenario for you and what does that *mean* to you?

If you want to defeat the dragon, you have to look it in the eye first. And I believe your dreams are worth fighting for.

I "CAN'T"

"I can't get to the gym today because it's too late." "I can't go to that networking event because I'm too tired." I can't sit down and write the next chapter because I have to call my mom". "I can't meditate every day because I don't have enough time." "I can't go to that workshop because I don't have enough money."

(By the way, not having enough time or money are our most common excuses for why we can't stick to our goals.)

The problem with buying into this bullshit is that these excuses keep us in victim mode. When you say you "can't" it suggests that you have no control over the situation at all.

Which by the way, is NOT true. Now yes, it's true you can't control other people, the economy, the president's tweets, or all of your life's circumstances. But you CAN control your reaction to what's happening in your life. You have control over your attitude and responses. AND, by making one little shift, you can take back the reins of control once again.

It's time for a reality check.

How? Replace I "can't," with I "*won't*".

Ouch.

Oh, but that four-letter word...

But, saying I "won't" is more truthful, isn't it?

It's not that you don't have enough time to meditate every day. The truth is, you just "don't want" to carve out that time from your busy day. Finding the time will take work and require you to sacrifice doing something else.

It's not that you can't get to the gym, it's that you "don't want" to go to the gym. You don't want to have to deal with all the effort that it will take, not to mention the potential muscle aches you'll feel tomorrow.

Because if it's really important to you, you'll make the time and find the money to get it done. So, it's not a matter of "I can't".

It's a matter of "I won't".

Here's a great assignment to bust those lies.

Write down at least 10 of your excuses (Again, don't do this in your head). This shouldn't take that long because we all know our excuses by heart. So, stop right now, pull out your journal and actually write them down.

This is not a "See, I *am* a loser destined to be a failure" expedition. This is not something to beat yourself up about. This is part of being human and we ALL have tons of excuses that seem like really good reasons for not getting things done. Yes, even moi!

So, write out your top 10 excuses.

Then ask yourself. "okay, let's say that wasn't an issue, what could I do...?"

For example, let's say, "I can't get to the gym because I don't have enough time" is your fave excuse. So, if that wasn't an issue, what *could* you do?

- Set your alarm for earlier in the morning

- Gather your gym clothes and have them ready the night before (I know people who've slept in their gym clothes so in the morning they just got up and went to the gym!)

- Set a time to meet someone else at the gym (workout buddies work!)

- Bring your gym clothes with you in the morning and then go straight from work

- Look into classes being offered and schedule

them into your week

- Check out YouTube for FREE tutorials and classes which eliminates the time needed to even go to the gym.

Do you see how there are actually many ways to "create" time by having a plan of attack? (and yes, I have an entire chapter devoted to this coming up)

What about the money excuse? "I can't take that workshop because I don't have enough money". Really? I smell some BS...what if it wasn't an issue? What 'could' you do?

- You could contact the organization and work out a payment plan

- Ask the organization if they need volunteers which could help you lower your attendance fee or even eliminate it

- You can make your own coffee and/or pack a lunch for work to save on overpriced meals out (not eating out saves a ton of money...)

- Could you pick up a side job? ...Maybe drive for Uber or create an account on Task Rabbit.

- All of us have too much junk...do you have something you could sell on Ebay or Craigslist, or at a local consignment shop?

Those are just a few ways you can create extra money for something, if you *really want it*.

Don't let that four letter word "can't" get in your way. Swap it out for the truth. "I won't" and get honest about why you're stuck. Then take back the reins of control by calling out your excuses and replacing them with concrete actions.

Yet another BS phrase we use as an excuse:

"Once I've"

> *"Waiting for Mastery is Foolish!"*
> - Tara Bliss

This is another common excuse many of us use to hold ourselves back. We think we have to have figured everything out before taking action (which by the way leads to overwhelm which is up next).

But likely, whatever your goals are, be it writing a play, redoing your bathroom, finding a new job...you probably have some skills already and can get started right away. That's not to say that at some point you won't need to learn more skills or get help. You likely will. But, that's not a reason to not start TODAY.

The truth is, no ideas have ever been perfectly executed and nobody is ever truly prepared for the future.

Some of the most common excuses I hear:

"Once I've lost weight, I'll _____."

"Once I've gotten certified, I'll _____."

"Once I've gotten over my past, I'll _____."

Usually anytime we say, "Once I've" we are making a big excuse. And this is a sneaky one because there may be partial truth to it.

For example, depending on your goals, weight loss might be a good idea. But, I'm sure there are some steps you can take towards your goals WHILE losing the weight. You don't need to have your weight where you want it to get started today.

Is getting certified as a yoga instructor a good idea for being a successful yoga teacher? Of course it is. BUT, if that is your desire, then you are likely already doing lots of yoga! And, you could probably find some people to practice your teaching skills with.

Waiting to get over your past? Good luck with that one!

Here are two examples of women whom I not only admire, but I've received unlimited inspiration and healing from. And, they both started without waiting to figure it all out first.

Geneen Roth is a best selling author and world renowned speaker on the topic of emotional eating. She also has healing retreats all over the world for women struggling with their various eating disorders. She started by getting together with 5 or so women, charging them $10 a meeting, and inviting them to discuss their issues with food. She did not wait to get any formal training, and, she did not wait to figure out her own issues with food...she just put it out there and the women showed up. Now, she is known as *the* expert on emotional eating.

Tara Bliss is also a best selling writer, spiritual life coach, and inspirational speaker. She also offers web-classes that help women from all over the world. How did she create all this? With a blog. What was her plan? Well, at the time she decided to create an on-line space, she lived in Japan and was picking oranges for a living. She had no clue what she was intending for her future, she just knew, she wanted to share her stories with other women and created the now famous "Such Different Skies" blog. She wrote her stories, shared pictures, favorite music, put up videos...and people started taking notice. Now, she speaks all over the world, has a thriving essential oil business, and coaches women on a global scale.

And, personally, I've asked many of the successful people I've met, "When did you know you were ready to start?"

Usually I get a good laugh from that question and the answer is almost always, "If I'd waited to *feel* ready, I never would have started!"

So, listen in to your self talk...are the words "Once I've..." a part of your inner dialogue?

Overthinking and Overwhelm...Just Another Excuse

This is another common issue for so many of us. We paralyze ourselves by thinking and rethinking "There is too much to do" or "Where do I start?" We brood and brood on this until next thing we know, we are spaced out or numbing out with food or Facebook. By the time we awaken from our overthinking haze, we are too exhausted and confused to take any actions at all.

What we are failing to see is that *not knowing the answers* can be an *opportunity* to trust your intuition.

'Mastin Kipp', inspirational speaker, best selling author, and regular guest on Oprah's "Soulful Sunday's", started his road to recovery by: making his bed. At the time, he was addicted to pain killers and living in his friend's tiny back house which was basically a room and a bathroom. He was completely broke and unemployed...again. Finally he said "enough" and decided to change his life. He had no clue where to begin or what to do. But he decided that he didn't care that he had no clue! He looked around his tiny room, which was a disaster (much like his entire life)... and he started with what was right in front of him...his bed. That was 'step one' of his recovery. From there he went on to have one of the most inspirational and successful blogs "The Daily Love", and was on "The Oprah Winfrey Show" within a few years.

Having a plan, some education, and good mentoring is always great when embarking on anything we choose to do. But not having those things does not mean you have *nothing*. It doesn't mean you can't start right now.

Indecision and lack of clarity are not reasons to stay stuck or allow ourselves to get overwhelmed. In fact, taking action despite the unanswered questions will help you create more faith in yourself. (Nike's slogan: "Just Do It" might be your new mantra!)

Look back at when you were a teenager. A lot of us thought we knew *everything* when we were teenagers and of course now, we look back and laugh. *But,* notice that not knowing the outcomes of our actions didn't stop us from trying new things and taking risks. We still had the same fears of failure and humiliation that we have now as adults. But, in our teens, we went for it anyway.

Don't worry! I am in no way suggesting we behave like teenagers again! (I never want to go back!!!) But what many of us lose as we get older, is our ability to tolerate the discomfort of not 'knowing' the outcome. We are willing to go for it...but only if there is a guarantee of success.

We also know that there are no guarantees in life so where does that leave us?

Stuck in the rut of indecision and overwhelm.

The only way to get out of that rut is to take a step out. Knowing the right way out is not necessary. Taking action *is*.

And, the more steps you take, the more confident you will feel in your decision making skills. You will more easily trust your intuition and spend less and less time stuck in indecision. You will also realize more quickly when you have made the wrong decision and will be able to get back on track more easily.

And yes, you will be off track sometimes. What's important is how fast you can get back ON track. And that takes action...not waiting for clarity or some guarantee that your actions will work.

Is there something in front of you that you can do *right now*?

But, I'm Just Not Feeling Inspired... Sniff, Sniff

"Don't wait for Inspiration...It comes while one is working." -Henri Matisse

"You miss 100% of the shots you don't take." -Wayne Gretzky

This is yet another trap many of us fall into...thinking we need to first be inspired before taking action. But waiting for that spark creates tension and unrealistic expectations that ultimately lead to us doing nothing at all.

If professional athletes were waiting to feel "in the mood" to practice, they would never make it to the pros.

If stock brokers pondered their lack of excitement to get up early, they'd hit the snooze button and never make the money they could.

If life coaches waited to feel inspired before writing a book...well...I think you get the point. For years, I've published new material every two weeks for my website and that takes effort! And rarely do I sit down full of excitement to write about something that inspired me. Sometimes, yes. But mostly, no. (sorry...) I show up in front of my computer, pick a topic or a quote, and get the work done. And usually after less than a minute, I'm 'inspired' to write at least a full draft or two.

The act of "waiting to feel inspired" shuts off your communication with your creative mind. You end up with an unrealistic expectation of creating something wonderful. That's a lot of pressure! And, creativity comes from the right side of the brain. But that side cannot be accessed unless you are already absorbed in your work. In other words, the left side of your brain sits your ass down to work, then, after a few minutes, the right side begins to share it's ideas.

So you can see that waiting for inspiration is actually killing the likelihood of it showing up at all!

One trick to getting yourself to show up is to shorten the time you intend to do your work. Like I said previously, make it easy to succeed. Setting your goal to work on your project for only 15 minutes is a great idea. I mean, come on, everyone can find 15 minutes to work on what they are passionate about! If you work longer, fab again! But even if all you do is 15 minutes, it's still better than 0 minutes because of you putting extra pressure on yourself.

Calling Even More Bullshit on Yourself

We all have 'stories' as to why we 'can't' do this or 'don't have' that. The truth is, those beliefs are just more excuses. Ouch, really? Let me prove my point. (I'm sorry if I sound harsh, but some of us need to get real.)

Write out your story or beliefs about why you can't just go for it. Again, this won't take you long because like in the previous exercises, you know your stories by heart by now.

"I'm too fat." "I'm too old." "I'm too young." I'm under qualified." I'm not smart enough." "It's always been that way." "I'm weak." "I'm not a lucky person." "I don't deserve it." "I'm lazy." "I'm a fraud." "I'm damaged."

...You get the point.

Write out all the "why's" you can't go for it.

Truth bomb...You are keeping those stories because you are getting something out of them. They are serving you in some way. How? By keeping you safe. Once again, your mind is finding yet another way to avoid the fear of the unknown.

And, as long as you believe your excuses to be true, you will never follow through on your commitment to take action. You'll stay safe in your comfort zone and miss out on what dreams could have come true for you. Regardless of how much you hate those beliefs, you are clinging to them for dear life.

As promised, I'll prove it to you.

Reread your story and imagine your best friend telling you that it's total crap...not true at all. Write out your response. How much do you defend your story? List all the reasons why you know you're right.

All the past experiences that you've had that prove that you are 'damaged' etc.

The more fear you have around dropping that belief, the more you will defend it and hang onto it.

I have worked with many people in all walks of life and I've never seen anyone create lasting change until they first dealt with their BS stories.

I've seen patients literally re-injure themselves because they couldn't fathom a life without pain! I had one client who actually called herself 'Calamity Jane' like it was a badge of honor. What a waste.

So, write out your bullshit story. Defend the crap out of it and notice the fear that it brings up in you. What are you afraid will happen if you don't believe this lie and instead throw it out all together?

THEN...off the top of your head, write out those fears. Overthinking won't help. As stupid as they may seem, fire them off and get them on the page.

Take a few deep breaths when you're done. That was big.

Now, come back to that list of fears.

Are you going to let them stop you?

Avoid falling into the trap of "I should have known that...", or "I should have gotten over this by now..." According to who?!? (By the way, that's another BS belief.)

Again, are you willing to let those fears decide your future?

I hope your answer is NO.

If you said 'no', then go DO ONE THING that will pull you forward towards your goals right now. Take action now.

Finally, be gentle with yourself after you've done this process. It's powerful and will likely bring up a lot of uncomfortable feelings. That's normal. Fear is something we all avoid feeling yet need to examine in order to move beyond it.

What I love about this process is that now you are being completely honest with yourself. Knowing your personal fears is a powerful tool to overcoming them. They are no longer lurking in your subconscious. They are out in the open for you to challenge.

So again, write out your Bullshit story, defend the crap out of it, write out your fears that come up, and question them honestly.

Are you waiting for permission?

Remember when you were a kid in school? You had to have your parent's permission to take field trips, miss classes, etc. You had to ask permission to speak, go to the bathroom...you even needed permission slips to walk down the halls when classes were in session.

(I actually got busted for writing fake permission slips in junior high! Well, the teachers never figured out it was me, but one of my friends did get in trouble for the fake slip. I spelled Tuesday wrong...I never was very good at spelling...)

Our childhoods were a time when we really didn't have control over very much of our lives, certainly not in school. And unless we were allowed to make some decisions for ourselves at home, we were never given the tools to have agency over our lives.

And now as adults, some of us are still waiting for permission to express our power, our creativity, and our voices. Look at how many women stayed quiet for so long before the '#me too' movement began? It took many brave women (and men) to come forward and share their experiences regardless of whether they were "permitted" to do so. And their bravery started a movement that has only just begun.

So, what are you afraid will happen if you speak up and claim your power? For me, the answer has always been, "I don't want to offend anyone." That has kept me quiet and safe time after time.

What about you? Are you afraid of losing love? Feeling embarrassed? Triggering anger in others? These are all valid fears and very common.

No one is suggesting we lie to ourselves and say we're not afraid. We all are. And sometimes with very good reason.

So instead, let's try having a different perspective on those fears. Add a few words…"I'm willing"

For example, "I don't want to offend anyone" becomes, "I'm willing to stifle my power so I don't offend anyone."

Fear of embarrassment? I'm willing to squander my talents so I don't feel embarrassed or embarrass anyone else."

Fear of losing love? "I'm willing to play it safe and dim my inner light so I don't lose the ones I love."

How does that feel? If you're like me, that feels icky and makes you a little angry. My response is, "Screw that! I'm not keeping my mouth shut just so others aren't offended!"

Where else do you need permission? Are you avoiding exploring your abilities to paint, or sing, or dance? Are you waiting for permission to take a day off for self care? Are you waiting for permission to love and appreciate yourself right now as you are?

I'll ask you again...What are you afraid of? What do you think will happen if you own that you are lovable just as you are? Are you afraid people will laugh at you or make fun of you? Are you afraid you'll go to the other extreme and become conceited with an inflated ego?

Rephrase your fears. "I am willing to deny my lovability so that people don't think I'm conceited". Ouch. No! Love yourself right now!

And, riddle me this, Batman...Who do you think is going to give you this permission in the first place?

You know the answer to that...YOU. No one else is sitting around waiting to give you permission to shine. It's up to YOU.

So here it is, your own permission slip to be exactly who you want to be and do exactly what you want to do. You have full permission to be your most powerful, creative, lovable self.

Today's Date:

I, _____,
am giving permission to myself to:
_____ and

_____.

_____

Signature

I suggest you type out your own and make copies. Fill one out every day, and post it where you will see it often. Permission slips are a powerful symbol from our childhood. Taking this action every day will have a profound effect on your life and give you the courage to take action despite your fears.

No more waiting for permission. Its time to start claiming your power. Now.

Exercises to go back and review:

- Why do you stop yourself, and do you fear joy?

- How do you sabotage yourself? (overwhelm, waiting for inspiration..)

- Notice your excuses when you say "I can't..." and "Once I've..." and "I'm willing..."

- Your BS story

- Permission Slip

Chapter Four

Flags of Gratitude Garden Craft

Gratitude is a number one stress reliever and has been proven to make us happier (more of that in the upcoming chapter.) Why not turn that Gratitude into something tangible and fun?

You will need:

- Fabric (you can do various patterns or just plain white...it's your garden, you get to choose!)

- Scissors

- Craft glue (Elmer's glue works just as well)

- Small wood square dowels (available at Michaels, Amazon, etc)

- Acrylic or other oil based paints

- Paint brushes

- Oil-based white pen (I love the look of white lettering vs black...it makes your words 'pop')

- Your gratitude list...so you can collect:

- Pictures of people, pets, and whatever visuals represent what you're grateful for

- Fake sand

- Vase or pot if you don't have a private garden space

- Glitter (optional, of course!!!)

Making your Flags of Gratitude:

1.   First, you will cut your flags. Cut fabric approximately 11" x 5" or to the size you like. Lay your fabric so the wrong side is facing you. Place the dowel in the middle of fabric and glue the fabric pieces together folding them with the dowel in the middle. Let glue dry.

2.   Using your acrylic pain, paint your flags however you want to. Make them as colorful and bright as you like. They do not have to match. Have fun, as if you were a child playing with finger paints.

3.   Let them dry completely (this may take a day or so...).

4.   Using your white pen, write on the flags all that you are grateful for and glue your pictures on various flags as well. You can also write directly on the pictures stating why you are grateful for them (Add glitter!).

5.   Then, find a special place in your garden and 'plant' the flags. If you don't have a garden, find a pretty pot   (or maybe a vintage one from a second hand store), fill it with dirt or fake sand, and plant the flags where you can admire them.

Attitude Adjustments

Strategies to live happier days while increasing the likelihood of our success.

How practicing being happy and confident can help you achieve your goals

Shawn Achor of Harvard has spent his life studying happiness and its relevance in corporate America as well as corporations around the world. Countless studies have been done to prove that happy workers not only perform better at their jobs, but actually create more profit for the companies they work for.

But, most of us are not CEO's of Fortune Five Hundred companies. So how can we use this research in practical ways to improve our own lives? After all, if it works for corporate America, couldn't it work for us?

Yes, it *can*! According to studies, the minimal amount of happy/confident experiences required to increase the likelihood of success, is 3 new experiences a day. But, these experiences must be specific to our own personal preferences. And these preferences are known as, our 'signature strengths'. (and you will likely discover an overlap with your 'signature emotions').

What does that mean, 3 new experiences a day? It means at least 3 times a day, you have to consciously engage in different things that make you feel confident and happy. Some examples: admiring the pretty flowers in someone's garden, complimenting a co-worker, finding the humor in a situation, being grateful for a good nights sleep, learning something new, reviewing your previous successes... The key is, you have to figure out what makes YOU happy and confident and start looking for opportunities to experience more of those feelings on a daily basis.

So what makes you happy? Humor? Love of learning? Creativity? Gratitude? Curiosity? Sit for a few minutes and remember the times you were genuinely happy. What was going on? What were you doing? Did you find something funny about the situation? Were you engrossed in learning something new? Write down all the activities that contributed to your happiness.

And, when did you feel successful? What were you doing and how did it feel? For example, maybe you got the client because you 'just clicked with them' and shared the same sense of humor. Then 'humor' and 'engaging with others' should go on your list of signature strengths. (If you want to get scientific about it, go to viasurvey.org and fill out their survey...its fun, fast, and free!)

Some of you still might think that pain and struggle is the only way to success and all this happiness talk is nonsense. Well, just to inspire you even more, here is an interesting experiment done by Margaret Shih at Harvard. She gathered a group of Asian women of the same IQ and administered a math test. But, before the test, she told them that because they were women and generally women are bad at math, she didn't expect great scores. Not surprisingly, the women scored low. Then, a different test was administered to another similar group of women. Only this time she told them that because they were Asian they were expected to do well because Asians are culturally better at math. You guessed it...they scored high!

Another test at Harvard, involving Doctors, proved that Doctors primed with happy feelings before seeing a patient, yielded more accurate diagnosis' than those Doctors simply going from patient to patient. I don't know about you, I'd rather have a happy Doctor see me the next time I'm sick!

Science has repeatedly proven that the happier and more confident you feel, the more likely you are to succeed. (and thus Corporate America has jumped on board because success = money!)

So...what if you primed yourself to feel confident before going into your job interview, pitching your project, sitting down to write, or dealing with your children? The key is to remember what makes *you* happy and confident.

Get your list of 3-5 things that you can do on a daily basis to feel great, and then do them every day. (I have my list posted front and center on my journal so I start every day feeling positive and confident...and what are my signature strengths, you might ask? Gratitude, Spirituality, Humor, Love, and Creativity. So my day starts with a Gratitude list...every day.)

Again, I repeat, practice them DAILY. And more importantly, practice them purposefully and consistently when faced with challenges.

But what if I'm naturally moody?

*A **great** daily habit to improve our dispositions*

We are all born with different personalities, preferences, inclinations and dispositions. There was a vast study done in the 1950's called the 'New York Longitudinal Study on mood and temperament'. They studied toddlers to predict the various temperaments each child would likely exhibit as an older child and further on in life.

And ask any parent with more than one child, they will tell you that they are all different...same parents, same upbringing, different sensibilities.

So what about those of us drawn to the "broodier" side of life? Some people seem to be "hard wired" to see the negative, the mistakes, the worst case scenario...is that you?

Or maybe you used to be pretty happy in general but life has just served you up platter of shitty life circumstances and you feel bummed out more days than not?

(Let me be clear, I'm talking about general malaise—not *clinical depression*. If you feel clinically depressed or suicidal, seek medical help immediately.)

Well, there is good news for those of you who tend to feel down. You can 'rewire' your brain to actively look for things that bring a smile to your face. It just takes daily practice.

> - Random Acts of Kindness have been proven to, over time, help elevate people's moods. That means, just doing something nice for someone else for no good reason, can nudge you out of a slump.

> - Physically moving your body in positive ways (dancing, singing, looking up at the sky, etc) has a psychological effect on your moods. So if you are staring at your feet feeling sad, look up! That sends a neuromuscular message to your nervous system to change its focus thus

changing your state from bummed, to uplifted.

But, my favorite way to rewire our brains to see the good, is:

-Keeping a Gratitude Journal (even if Gratitude wasn't one of your top Signature Strengths)

Everyday for the next 2 weeks, sit down with your journal and write about something good that happened to you that day. You have to come up with and write specifically about something *new* that happened to you... that you were grateful for...every day for at least 2 weeks.

As I've said, our brains love repetition and love feeling good. So, by repeating this action of positive journaling every day, your brain will start to look for more experiences for things to write about. Your brain can't help it! Remember it's wired to create habits! And, this habit happens to feel good...so your mind will have no choice but to want to reinforce it daily.

This may sound overly simplistic, until you give it a try. For some of us, at first, finding a good thing to write about might be a challenge. So, start small and easy. Did someone smile at you today? Did your car get you from point A to B without incident? Did you see a funny video on YouTube? You don't have to come up with monumental things that happened to you. Just write about something that made you smile, or laugh, or feel at peace. Stick with it for at least 2 weeks and then start to notice how much easier it is to remember the great things that happen every day.

And no need to wait until you're depressed to start this habit...I think we could ALL benefit from finding more gratitude in our lives.

I've said it before, I'll say it again: We all have the capacity to increase the sum joy in the world every minute of every day.

Despite our dispositions, we do have a choice.

Speaking of Choices...

Which Wolf Are You Feeding?

This conversation was widely shared soon after 9/11:

A grandfather and his grandson were talking. The grandfather said, "I have 2 wolves fighting inside of me. One is filled with anger, hate, violence and revenge. The other is filled with love, kindness, compassion, and forgiveness."

"Which one do you think will win?" asked the grandson.

"The one that I feed," replied the grandfather.

Stop and think about that for a second. Which wolf are you feeding these days?

Your self-talk, your values, and your beliefs affect how you react to your world. And your beliefs are created by thinking the same thoughts over and over again until you 'believe' they are true. Which means it's important to know what you're thinking.

When you are thinking attack thoughts, you are feeding the wolf of hate and negativity. Just like, when you are thinking loving thoughts you are feeding the wolf of compassion and kindness. I'm going to make the assumption that most of us would prefer to feed the wolf of kindness.

Before we go into more detail on managing our thoughts, I want to invite you to also monitor your social media feed. This is the one area where many people feel compelled to dump verbal sewage and spew it out at the world without taking any responsibility for the ugliness they are contributing. I strongly urge you to take several deep breaths before posting hate on the web. Again, which wolf are you feeding if you actually post that tweet.

What is the most generous assumption I can make (and still acknowledge my feelings)?

There is a fabulous book called "The Four Agreements" by Don Miguel Rusiz (If you haven't read it, do so!) It's basically stating that if you follow the "four agreements", you will have less conflict in your life.

One of the agreements that has always stuck with me is "Make No Assumptions".

Let's face it...some of our assumptions, mainly our assumptions about other people, can be harmful and counter productive.

Think back to a time in the past week or so, when you had a disagreement with someone that left you feeling bad afterwards. Maybe you felt judged, belittled, embarrassed, hurt... Take a moment now to see if you can recall what your thoughts were at that time.

"He thinks I'm stupid", "She thinks she's better than me", "He doesn't care about me", "She's only in it for herself"...etc, etc, etc. Just notice the thoughts.

Now, ask yourself, 'can I know for certain, that my thought is true?'

Usually when our buttons get pushed, we are diving deep into a swarm of thoughts that have little truth and even less relevance to the situation at hand.

But, how can you stop the story once it's started?

By interrupting it.

Go back to the situation you recalled. You've already noticed your thoughts. Now, acknowledge your feelings (hurt, angry, etc). But, ask yourself "What is the most generous assumption I can make right now?"

Assuming "she's only in it for herself" probably isn't the most generous assumption you could make. What else "could" be going on?

Can you know for certain, "He thinks you're stupid?" What's a different assumption you could make?

Making a generous assumption doesn't mean you let people get away with behaving badly or that you stop setting boundaries. Making a generous assumption helps *you* behave in a better way for *you*. It helps you side-step your old beliefs and allows space for your mind to come up with a solution rather than an attack.

And yes, you have to practice asking yourself this question until it becomes automatic.

When someone blows the stop sign..."What is the most generous assumption I can make right now?" Sure, they may be a self-centered jerk, or, maybe they just got news of an emergency...

When your client is late..."What is the most generous assumption I can make right now?" Well, they might have no respect for you or your time, or maybe they had an issue with traffic or their room-mate took their keys by accident.

When someone cuts ahead of you in line, "What is the most generous assumption I can make right now?" They might be totally unconscious and self-absorbed, but maybe they just didn't see you.

By asking this question, you are not negating the possibility that they are unconscious, selfish, etc. But you are creating the possibility that a slightly less harsh belief could also be true. And that will likely help you react in a less confrontational way. Thus... alleviating some potential anger and stress.

Then when bigger things happen like your friend or partner or boss snaps at you..."What is the most generous assumption I can make right now?" will be a natural thought before you respond.

Attack Thoughts...How to Transform Your Anger into Peace

Sometimes, someone does something that hits all our angry buttons at once and we not only fly off the handle, we hold onto that anger and stoke it like a fire. Anything can set us off if we're triggered the right way...unconscious drivers, obnoxious coworkers, demanding family members...personal or not, there are times when we get overly upset and feel the need to rant and rave. (And your generous assumptions just aren't going to be enough!)

Whether it's your boss, spouse, parent, child...we all have had the experience of being so angered that we start an entire make believe fight with them in our mind. Usually this involves you feeling vindicated in some way and almost always leaves them feeling ashamed and feeling horribly remorseful.

If this sounds familiar, it's important to take a "time out" for yourself and notice the endless loop you are in. Whether it's in your head, or on the computer as you rewrite an angry email over and over...however it's transpiring, notice that you are stuck in an anger rut. (And don't send the email!)

Then, ask yourself how *you* are feeling. If you want to prove them wrong, that's an indication that you feel you were let down, judged, or hurt in some way. It's a signal that somehow, your expectations

79

were not met. Notice if you want to make them feel ashamed and remorseful. The desire to hurt someone else almost always comes out of our own feelings of being hurt.

First question to ask yourself: will confronting this person help me in any way? Will it open up the channels for communication, or will it lead to more negativity and failed communications?

If there is something you can do about the problem, I recommend taking at least 3 deep breaths. Then, respond respectfully and proactively rather than making a negative knee jerk reaction . And, if you feel like you will likely still overreact, go home and address it tomorrow after you've had a good night's sleep.

If, however, you know you are being irrational and want to let this go, there are a few things you can do to transform your feelings of upset into a more peaceful mindset.

> #1. Ask yourself: "Do I want to keep these attack thoughts? Can I find the place inside of me where I can genuinely say ...I don't want to feel this way towards them?"

Then ask:

> #2. Am I WILLING? Am I honestly willing to give up making them wrong over and over again in my head? Another way to ask that question is...what do I have to give up in order to let those thoughts go? What am I hanging onto?

Chances are, you will have to spend a good amount of time answering these questions. This is again, where journalling can be a huge help. It keeps your mind focused in the present rather than drifting back into your anger pattern. You can clearly see your assumptions and your thoughts and then more easily find the place inside you that's ready and willing to drop this negative thinking.

Then what? Let it go. Some people visualize their thoughts in a balloon floating away. Or drifting down a stream or getting swept up in a breeze. For some people, just stating out loud "I am willing to let this go. I am now letting this go." is enough to feel peace.

However you do it, just do it. And then, when those feelings crop up again, (because they usually pop up again a few more times), you can kindly remind yourself that it's actually in your best interest not to dwell on those thoughts anymore. You've examined your feelings on the matter and would rather feel peace, than anger.

Again, I always like to start small. Start with the person that was so engrossed in their smartphone that they failed to look before they stepped in front of your car. Yeah, that unconscious idiot...start with your attack thoughts about them. Go through the process of asking if keeping these attack thoughts are helping you feel good. Find out where within you, you could be willing to let those thoughts go. And then, let them go...

When the Shit Hits the Fan...

I'm going to say it like it is...sometimes things suck. And sometimes they suck so much, we feel like we will never feel good again. Death of loved ones, sudden unemployment, serious illness, car accidents, hurricanes, earthquakes...a lot can go wrong that we have no control over.

This is why knowing your "personal signature emotions" is vital. (remember that section? if you skipped it, go back and read it now...)

You might be wondering, what good does knowing these emotions do for you when you are NOT feeling anywhere near those feelings. Maybe you want to feel vibrant and full of energy but you have the flu. Maybe you want to feel unstoppable and in sync with the universal flow but your flight got delayed overnight thanks to a snowstorm. Maybe you want to feel abundant and free but you just got nailed with a huge overdue IRS payment and will have to borrow more money just to get ahead of it.

First, when things turn crappy, don't lie to yourself. If you have the flu, you likely feel like you have the plague. Admit it. You feel like shit on a stick.

Then, rather then wallowing in that feeling, ask yourself:

What can I do right now to help myself feel *closer* to how I *want* to feel? Is there a baby step you can take to feel *closer* to how you want to feel?

> *"Life is 10% what happens to me and 90% of how I react to it"*
> -Charles Swindoll

How we look at the situation is where we can actually take more control over our lives. Having a week long pity party or brooding over the shit storm you're going through will only keep you in the storm. At a certain point, you need to leave the storm zone.

The way out of the storm is your attitude. And, by finding ways to feel a little bit closer to your "personal signature emotions," you are more likely to be in a better mood.

Remember, you may not get to decide what lessons life gives you, but you *do* get to decide how you'll behave and what you will focus on.

Is it possible to bring some humor or lightness into the situation? Despite the crap you're dealing with, can you still be grateful for something? Is there something creative or loving you can offer at the moment? Again, what can you do that is likely to help you feel a little closer to your signature emotions?

Because *you* get to decide how you show up for your life. Even when things go sideways.

And I want to share a personal experience I had as a very young, very new Pilates instructor. I was teaching a semi-private with about 4 clients. One of them, Diane, a woman of about 50, came in for the session in tears. She had been to visit her mother...who didn't recognize her. Her mother's Alzheimer's had advanced and she didn't recognize Diane at all. Another client, Lenny, had lost both his mother and sister to cancer earlier that year. Here were his words of advice that I'll never forget...

"You can't control the situation, how she's feeling or behaving or any of it. Eventually it will end. Eventually, she'll pass away. And then, all you will have left is how you 'showed up' for her. That's all you can control and all you really have. You get to decide how you'll show up."

Having experienced the loss of many important people in my life, including my father, I'm so grateful I heard those words back then. I was able to show up to all of my losses with some amount of grace and patience, and gratitude and faith. I hope you take that advice to heart, for whatever crisis you may have to deal with.

Reclaiming our Sovereignty to Let Go of Envy

Sovereignty is a word being tossed all around the self-help world these days. And that's a good thing. Our world, our communities, and our relationships need to evolve away from the guru mentality and more towards taking responsibility for ourselves and our choices.

As we gain more wisdom, the old model of us being the dutiful student at the feet of our masters has to dissolve. Our new relationship to leadership, in all of its forms, should feel more like we are standing shoulder to shoulder with those that we admire.

The old model breeds disempowerment and often leads to envy. We become envious of our role models, friends, and public figures. And in my opinion, envy is one of the causes of the high levels of anxiety many of us struggle with daily.

When we envy or overly admire someone, we are subconsciously deciding we *can't* have what they've got. We often have elaborate stories as to why "poor me isn't as successful, attractive, wealthy (fill in the blank) as they are." As a result, we play small in the shadow of our worship of these 'successful' people or ideals.

Anything that puts you at the bottom of a pedestal creates the opportunity for envy...which always leads to disempowerment.

I'm not saying we have nothing left to learn from other people. I believe the opposite is true. But, I am saying our *approach* needs to change to a more equal playing field. How we handle ourselves and our own power is what will create change in those relationships. And, it will also change how we learn from others.

What if, instead of looking at someone and thinking, "oh, she's so in touch with her inner power...I wish I were more like her," we looked at that person and thought, "oh, she's showing me how I too can be in touch with my inner power. She's reflecting something I'm not yet seeing in myself."

Isn't that thought more accurate?

If you are hooked into envying people, then obviously they are triggering something in you that is either dormant or undernourished. After all, you're not preoccupied with people you don't like. You envy people for something they have, that you want.

For example, if you are envious of your friend who just dropped 10 pounds, ask yourself what she's revealing to you that you are yet to accept about yourself. Maybe she made her health a priority and you are still struggling with your bad eating habits. Maybe she's showing you that, if you choose to, you too have the capacity to set a clear goal and stick to it.

Maybe you are admiring an inspirational speaker yet feeling bad about your personal progress on your own healing path. What might they be revealing to you? That you have the power to step up your game or to be more disciplined with your practices? Maybe they are illuminating your need to take more responsibility for your actions.

Because when you see those qualities as something you could cultivate in yourself, you claim your power back. You own your whole being without being at the mercy of someone else's success or wisdom. You stop being envious and become proactive in the creation of your life.

And when you can claim and own all of your power, even where you may still be struggling...*that* is the definition of sovereignty. And the more you live from that energy, the more you instinctively help others to live in their sovereignty. You will start to become aware when others are "looking up to you" rather than just taking a cue from your actions. You can more easily discern what is "their stuff" and what is "your stuff." And in owning "your stuff" you automatically empower them with an opportunity to do the same. It gives both of you the freedom and space to communicate openly.

So, take a look at the relationships in your life. Where are you putting your power at the base of a pedestal? Who are you envious of and why? Imagine standing shoulder to shoulder with that person...what are they showing you about what's possible for you? Where are you giving your power away? Where, in you, could you cultivate that which you are envious of?

Making this shift will absolutely change your life. It might change your thoughts about why you eat what you eat. It might change your thoughts about your wardrobe, how to approach your next conversation with someone, what books you read and who you get advice from. It will change your personal relationships as well as your global ones....In a good way. You will be reclaiming your power, reclaiming your sovereignty and simultaneously you'll be creating a world where others can claim their's too.

Setting and Enforcing Healthy Boundaries... Another Aspect of Sovereignty

This has been a life long lesson for me. Having grown up in a house with zero boundaries, I was never taught their importance. Or, for that matter, how to effectively set healthy boundaries and then enforce them.

If this resonates for you, don't worry. You CAN learn to set healthy boundaries. You CAN learn to enforce them. Although it might be uncomfortable in the beginning, setting boundaries is crucial to supporting your personal power.

There is a misleading perception these days... "be open, be inclusive, don't judge", etc...no matter what. Sure, we all agree that being nonjudgemental is a good thing. But not if someone is taking advantage of you or walking all over you. There is nothing spiritual or enlightened about being a doormat.

Another way of looking at boundaries, is seeing them as tools to ensure your standards are being respected. In other words, you haven't lowered the bar for other people. You hold them to the standards you expect, or move on. They know where you stand and can decide for themselves if the relationship works for them...and visa versa. Your job is to be clear and consistent.

The best way I have found to learn this skill is by modeling someone who is good at it. Studying someone who has mastered a skill you desire is a great way to learn. So, for example, if you want to learn how to be more comfortable with networking...you could find someone who's already comfortable with it and join them for some networking events. Then, watch their behavior and start behaving that way yourself. It may feel awkward at first, but it works. (Just like as children, we modeled our parents...there is a reason we sound just like our mothers sometimes!)

This works for any behavior you want to learn.

I didn't get really comfortable and capable with boundaries until I started working in a doctor's office as a rehabilitative Pilates Instructor.

Dealing with people in pain is challenging. Being in chronic pain is exhausting. And, some patients have more difficult personalities than others. So, setting boundaries became crucial for me in order to maintain my own personal sanity. And let me add, many of these people tried to test my boundaries or ignore them altogether. But I stayed firm...once I got comfortable enforcing them.

Fortunately the office manager, was outstanding at setting boundaries. He too had to learn this skill years ago, but he was clearly confident and capable now! I remember gawking at him several times in absolute amazement... "You can do that?" I remember thinking, "You can just say, 'No?" Without a bunch of excuses and apologies???" He was amazing.

I studied him like a hawk. And eventually, I became very clear about my boundaries, despite how uncomfortable it was at first.

Some personal examples:

- Session times: Some people are chronically late or just don't respect your time. I got really good at ending exactly on time. I didn't care if they were late...we ended on time. I had one patient show up still eating her breakfast which wasted 20 minutes of our session. I watched her eat...I still ended on time. And when she complained, I reminded her what time our session started, and that it was her choice to eat for the first 20 minutes. Our session was scheduled for one hour...not an hour and 20 minutes.

- Cancelation policy: Sometimes people think they are exempt from this policy which I clearly state, and put in writing. I insure I get paid in advance so if they cancel last minute, I'm still getting paid. My policy is my policy and if they don't like it, they can work with someone else. (I do make exceptions for people with chronic, painful health issues.)

Another boundary I learned to set was how to 'hold space' for people. By that I mean, someone could be struggling physically or emotionally, and rather than hooking into their emotions, I quietly, compassionately, observed them. I witnessed their pain...without getting personally involved with it. (And I wouldn't do any good as a life coach if every time a client got upset, I took on their pain...)

I think this boundary, 'holding space' is an important one for everyone to learn. Because, yes, people want to be seen, heard, and understood. But we can offer people that compassion and simultaneously keep our own sovereignty by staying in our own emotions and not hooking into theirs.

I repeat...We can be unrelenting in minding our own energy and emotions, and still compassionately observe the pain of others.

This is especially important now due to our current events. We are bombarded daily with all the terrible things happening in our world. If we allow ourselves to get sucked up into it, we'll burn out, break down, or self destruct.

Now more than ever we must set healthy boundaries and enforce them vigilantly. Especially when it comes to holding space and witnessing others.

Exercises to go back and Review:

- Signature Strengths

- Gratitude Journal

- Which Wolf are you Feeding?

- Generous Assumptions

- Attack Thoughts

- When the shit hits the fan

- Reclaiming our Sovereignty

- Setting and Enforcing Healthy Boundaries

Chapter Five

Lacy Candles Craft

I repurposed some lace table runners that were originally my Grandmother's. They were just sitting in my closet so I decided to repurpose them so they could be a part of the decor in my home. But you can always find lace at your local second hand store, or Joanne's, or Michaels (in the ribbon section)

<u>You will need:</u>

- Large votive candles

- Lace

- Glue (Elmer's glue if fine)

- Scissors

- Watercolor paints and water

- Paint brush

- Newspaper (to protect the surface you are painting on)

Making your Lacy Candles:

1.   Wrap the lace around the votive to measure how much you will need and then cut lace to that amount.

2.   Lay on newspaper.

3.   Paint the lace any color, colors you want.

4.   Allow to dry.

5.   Slather glue on the outside of your votive.

6.   Press lace onto votive and smooth it out so it covers the whole surface.

7.   Allow to dry.

Voila! Beautiful hand painted, lacy candles for your home.

Meditation And Mindfulness

"Life moves pretty fast. If you don't stop and look around once in a while, you could miss it."   - Ferris Bueller

By now you've heard the word "mindfulness" bashed around everywhere from yoga class to the supermarket. Yet are you practicing it? Not likely. Because most of us aren't even sure of what it means or how it can be useful.

So, because it has become so mainstream and yet not adequately defined, I'm actually going to rename the practice of mindfulness to "mind awareness". Because that name more truthfully describes the practice.

"Mind awareness" is exactly what it claims to be: becoming aware of what your mind is thinking. Another way of saying this is to 'pay attention to our thoughts, on purpose, in the present moment without judgment.'

In a nutshell, the goal is to disconnect from your thoughts and observe them, rather than associating and hooking into them.

By noticing your thoughts, you don't just take your thoughts as "truths" and act upon them. Instead you notice them, allow them to show up, but, you take no action based on them. You are now simply observing them. Thus, you are disengaging from the power they have over you. They are just thoughts. You decide whether to act on them or not.

Why is this so important and more than just a fad? Because we are all increasingly distracted, confused, and stressed out. Many of us are feeling depleted of our creativity and energy. The end result is that the stress we are enduring is damaging our health and mental abilities to succeed at our highest levels.

This is not some woo woo hippie thing. This is a fact. Here is a little evidence in case you are a doubter.

Earl Miller, a professor of neuroscience at MIT did a recent test on the effects of checking our email. He found that it can take your brain 15 - 20 minutes to get back to what you were working on before checking your inbox.

The University of Southern California did a study that discovered the estimated average American consumes 13 plus hours of media...*a day*!

And ask Google how much time we spend on just social media alone? 1 hour and 40 minutes...*a day*!

(And you complain you don't have enough time to be mindful and meditate???)

But before we dive into mind awareness further, we first have to talk about:

Meditation

We resist this discipline more than working out. We find time for Facebook, Pinterest, and Twitter! But we can't seem to carve out a few minutes for ourselves to do what we know will have immensely positive effects on not only our bodies, but our minds and spirits as well.

Why?

I think it's a combination of two things.

First of all, we make too big of a deal out of it. All meditation really is, is showing up for yourself, silently, for a few minutes a day. You can read studies about the optimal amount of time you should meditate, etc...forget all that. I know for me, my life didn't start to come together until I started meditating daily. Which meant sometimes...3 minutes. Seriously...3 minutes on some days. (and there are studies that show 3 minutes *is* enough...google it!)

So how come only a few minutes a day worked for me? Because I was showing up for myself regardless of how my day was going. I found at least 3 minutes (I aimed for more, of course) where *I sat, and silently connected to myself.* I put myself first in those moments. Which then created space in my mind for more compassion and respect for myself...both of which lead to peace of mind. It also opened the pathway for more creativity to come into my life...my etsy shop and my coaching business were both first 'thought of' while meditating.

Secondly, I think we aren't seeing the benefits of even small moments of meditation because we are looking for the wrong things. We've all heard that with consistent meditation, we can expect to see changes. Yet, we can meditate for a few weeks and it can seem like nothing is happening. In our culture, we expect instant gratification and improvements to be obvious. (Social media being a huge source of instant gratification and distraction, I might add.) But, with meditation, the changes happen slowly over time. Like a seed planted deep in the earth that somehow "magically" sprouts out into the sunshine one day. We know that seed has been working it's way up to the surface...slowly and silently without any judgement on the pace of its growth.

That's how meditation works. The shifts are subtle, yet ultimately powerful.

There are many forms of meditation. So, let's look at a specific way to meditate for mind awareness.

Set a timer for 3 minutes and sit comfortably with your eyes closed. Then, it's up to you as to how you want to practice. Some people follow their breath in and out. Some use a mantra that they silently repeat in their head. Some listen to pretty music. (My faves are included at the end of this book) What's most important is that you sit down and do it, not whether you're saying the right mantra.

You sit, for a chosen amount of time (remember, 3 minutes counts!), and notice when your thoughts distract you from your focus. Then, when you notice your mind has strayed, you simply return to your breath or mantra. That's it. Easy peasy.

And before you say you don't have enough time, I'll say it again...3 minutes every day is enough to see huge shifts in your life.

So, let's get back to how that translates into real life. When you practice noticing your thoughts when you are still and quiet, you will find it easier to notice your thoughts when you are busy living your life. And by noticing your thoughts, you can start to clear out some of the negative ones and replace them with something more positive. You will more quickly notice when you are being judgmental, impatient, and self critical. And because you are more conscious of those thoughts, you can then actively begin to cultivate more compassion.

And, the more you practice, the easier it gets.

- Schedule your time to sit and meditate. (Trust me on this, you won't do it unless you schedule a specific time.)

- Then, practice mind awareness throughout the day. Which you'll likely forget to do at first, as well.

Some of my clients have a reminder on their phone that goes off several times a day to remind them to observe their thoughts. Some post the words 'aware mind' in various places reminding them to be mind aware. Also try eating a meal without watching TV, or riding in the elevator without checking your phone. Just be, and notice your thoughts.

After a while, you won't need the reminders. But when first practicing this, I recommend doing something to help you remember throughout the day. After all, most of us are on auto pilot for a good amount of the time so remembering to shift into awareness can be challenging. So, set up some reminders to help you get into the habit of noticing your thoughts.

Harnessing the Power of our Subconscious Minds

"The secret of change is to focus all of your energy, not on fighting the old, but on building the new." -Socrates

"If you are struggling to achieve something, it is because your subconscious beliefs don't match your conscious desires." - Bruce Lipton

The subconscious mind has no emotions, no fears, no judgments. The subconscious mind simply looks to replicate that which it has been programmed to experience. So if your childhood taught you that it was best to stay quiet rather than rock the boat, then you are probably still silencing your voice and your power without being aware of it.

That old saying, "My buttons just got pushed..." is true. When you are reacting to something without thinking about it, your subconscious is in control and yes, your buttons are indeed being pushed.

So, how can we reprogram our subconscious to work with us rather than against us?

With a little prep, some repetition, and utilizing the moments we are drifting off to sleep or in meditation.

Remember your 'year in retrospect' that I had you write out? Go grab that now.

Now, let's add a few other specific beliefs to it...

Write out the answers to these questions:

- What actions or behaviors will I have taken when all of this comes true?

- What beliefs will I have about myself?

- What will I be saying to myself?

- Specifically, what will I be *doing*?

- And, what was eliminated?

- How will I act?

- How will I feel?

- How will it feel to live this way every day?

The clearer and more specific you are, the better.

Then, rewrite your 'year in retrospect'. Rewrite it incorporating your answers to the above questions. Then, re-record your new 'year in retrospect'.

You can then utilize this recording both in meditation and when you are falling asleep. As we fall asleep or when in deep meditation, our brain waves shift their pace and we are in a state similar to hypnosis. So by hearing your own voice celebrating your year of success, and defining your new beliefs and behaviors, you are programing your subconscious to make those images become your reality. Your subconscious will literally look for opportunities to make those new behaviors possible. Because again, that's all it's doing. It's replicating what it's been programmed to experience.

"Repetition is the mother of learning"
- Tony Robbins

So, listen to this recording throughout the day to further instill these new beliefs.

You can also harness this force for short terms goals as well. Let's say you have a big meeting tomorrow. You can do a quick voice recording, celebrating the fact that your meeting went great. Then, listen to it not only through-out the day but also before you fall asleep.

And, if you've tried but really can't get past listening to your voice, I recommend writing out that which you wish to manifest, in great detail. And then visualizing it fully before falling asleep and emotionally associating to it fully while meditating. Feel with every fiber of being, how it feels to already have what you want.

Also...if you are one of those people who wakes up a lot in the middle of the night, you can use that time to visualize the changes you want to see in your life. Again, you'll be reprograming your mind as you drift in and out of consciousness. (I did that after my dental surgery earlier this year. I spent my restless nights of interrupted sleep consciously visualizing the Doctor telling me that I had healed faster than normal. Which is exactly what happened. I was back to normal in one week. He said, it's at least 2-3 weeks for the average person to heal to the point I had. Yay...no more trips to the dental surgeon!)

Unplugging for the day

Do you ever stop and ask yourself if you are actually enjoying scrolling through Facebook, Instagram, Pinterest, the breaking news?

By being constantly connected, what are you actually contributing to and as a result, how much creativity are you letting slip by?

What would happen if you unplugged for an entire 24 hours? What might come up?

When I first did this, I realized very quickly how addicted I was to checking my email. I probably checked it 20 times a day. (at least!) By unplugging, I saw how many times I wanted to mindlessly check in and delete the junk mail. I also felt a little anxious. There was an underlying "F.O.M.O. (fear of missing out)" that I had never noticed before. Once that subsided, I noticed I actually felt LESS anxious than normal and was able to think more intuitively and allow for some creative ideas to surface that hadn't occurred to me before.

Here is a truth about addictive behavior: It gobbles up time you could be spending doing something else.

Another truth: It squashes creative ideas. You're simply too busy to notice them.

Years ago I coached the employees of a company through a weight loss challenge. They were divided into teams and each got a private phone session with me to help them strategize, etc. They all sent me emails telling me about themselves, their eating patterns, etc.

One man was morbidly obese and diabetic. When we spoke over the phone the first thing I suggested he do is pick up a hobby, preferably something where he used his hands. "When you give up your addiction to food, you will have so much free time on your hands....you'll need something to do." He started to laugh. Then told me he remembered being amazed at how much time he had after he'd given up drinking. He'd asked me if I'd ever been to AA and I said, "No, but I was a 2 pack a day smoker years ago...I had no idea how much time I was wasting taking 'smoke breaks'."

Same thing with technology addiction. Science has proven that we get a little 'hit' of dopamine every time we post online or get a 'like'. But that comes at a cost. It not only costs us our time, but our intuition and creative ideas as well. Not to mention the damage it's doing to our bodies.

In order for us to use our intuition and develop our creativity, we need to slow down and open ourselves up to our natural rhythms of thought and emotion.

This is true for our physical health as well. Practices like Yoga and Pilates are great for becoming present in our bodies. But not if your phone is on and you're checking texts between poses. No. You have to turn your phone OFF for that time period to experience the power of the present moment. (with one exception...Goat Yoga! Selfies are a Must!)

So here is my challenge to you. Schedule a day where you can go completely off line. If you are a parent, you'll still need to have your phone handy in case of an emergency. BUT, you do not have to check Facebook, Pinterest, Instagram, etc. You don't need to check your emails either. You can set up an auto response for the day...

"I'm unplugging for the day...talk to you tomorrow..." And, there are apps for blocking distractions if you know you can't do this alone: 'Digital Detach' for Android, 'StayFocused' for Google Chrome, and 'SelfControl' for macs are just a few of the apps out there.

Do this for one day this week. Don't just think about how it might feel...actually UNPLUG for 24 hours. Notice what that brings up for you? Notice if feelings of panic or loneliness come up. Maybe you feel depressed or bored. Or maybe you feel elated and free. Notice any creative or intuitive ideas that pop up and how much time you have to actually act on them.

Personally, I've made this a weekly habit that I now look forward to. It's a gift of freedom and creative expansion I give myself every week.

Using Mind Awareness as a Tool for Change

Let's say you're cutting out sugar but at the moment you are having a major sugar craving. Rather than fighting your urge, lean into it using your 'mind awareness' practice. How does this craving feel? Where do you feel it in your body? What are you thinking? What are you telling yourself right now? Get super curious and focus on what is actually going on in this moment.

Then, "ride the wave." This is a mindfulness technique which has you ask yourself the above questions, and feel what you're feeling as if riding a wave. You can even say, on a scale of 1-10...the size of this 'craving wave' is...And again, how does that feel?

Once you are present and mindful of what's going on, remind yourself of why you really want to create this change in the first place. (I discussed the importance of a strong "why" back in the goal setting chapter.) If you declared this to be the year you gave up sugar...why? You had great reasons for wanting to make this change. What are they? Remind yourself *why*.

Lastly, take action. If you're craving sugar, maybe have a cup of tea or kombucha. (you are still giving your mouth something to do!) Maybe the temptation is right in front of you...the waiting room candy jar! Can you move to a different seat where you can't so easily see the candy? Can you give your hands something to do like playing sudoku on your phone? If you are driving home and you know your favorite bakery is on the next block, *take a different street home!*

And, if you stay present and acknowledge how good you feel to have dodged the candy jar bullet, your brain will instinctively "memorize" that new behavior and *how good it feels*. Then, yet again, your brain will begin making a new habit. (which I talked about at length in chapter 2, Proven Strategies.)

If you are changing any behavior (breaking a bad habit or creating a new one) your willpower will be challenged at some point. So, *getting curious and present...noticing your thoughts...feeling your true desires...knowing your 'why's'...and then acting on them...*will give you the energy to make your new habits stick

Mindful Holidays

Oh, the holidays. Oh, family gatherings. How does it usually go for you? Raise your hand if you eat what feels like your entire body weight in holiday treats. Raise your hand if within five minutes of Thanksgiving dinner, you've already lost your shit with your relatives.

Okay, first of all, join the club. In my opinion, there is WAY too much emphasis on holidays and 'special occasions', and WAY too much pressure for all of us to do things perfectly.

The truth is, that's NEVER GOING TO HAPPEN. Perfection is impossible. So let's accept that. And instead of killing ourselves to get it right, let's find a way to actually enjoy these times without shame, anger, exhaustion, and an extra 5 pounds to lose.

This is a quick and easy way to interrupt your old patterns and instead become present and, yes, I'll say it, ' be mindful'. More importantly, you'll feel much more in control and less reactive to your Mother's nagging!

So, let's do it! The 'Presence Practice':

Feel your feet. How do they feel? Are you in shoes? Socks? Barefoot? Are they cold? Hot? If you had to describe how they felt what would you say...in detail...?

Okay, you just got present. You practiced another 'mindfulness' technique. Well done.

Here is the thing about our bodies and the 'presence practice'. Our bodies are living in the here and now. Second by second, breath by breath. Our bodies couldn't care less about what you did yesterday or, what you have to get done by the end of the week. Our bodies know nothing about shame, regret, or worry. Your critical mother? Our bodies have no thoughts about that either. They are simply here, right now.

So, when you are panicked about what to wear to the holiday party or worried about getting the table set in time for the guests, zone in on a part of your body and feel it fully. (And, FYI, this takes about 30 seconds so 'I don't have time' is, yet again, not an excuse.)

By just staying present with your body, your stress level is instantly reduced. And less stress means better thoughts. And most likely, more control over your reactions to other people... even Mom.

Practice this before the holidays arrive or the relatives come to visit. Get in the habit of doing this a couple of times a day, at least. And then, practice it incessantly when they're in town!

<u>Exercises to go back and Review:</u>

- 3 minute meditation

- setting timers/reminders to be 'mind aware'

- Utilize your subconscious to create change

- Unplug for the day

- Mindfulness to break bad habits

- Mindful holidays presence practice

Chapter Six

Make your own Fabric Craft

We've all done it...ruined our cozy wool sweater by throwing it in the washing machine in the hot water cycle.

But, if you do that on purpose, it's now fabric for you to make things with!

<u>You will need:</u>

- Wool sweaters (ideally 100% wool, cashmere, etc)
- Washing machine with agitator
- Lint roller
- Scissors, needle, thread...for whatever you decide to make when you're done!

Making Your Fabric:

If you have some wool sweaters that you are ready to take to the Goodwill, throw them in the hot water cycle and turn them into felt. You can also check out your local second hand stores to buy great wool and cashmere sweaters for very little cost.

Once you've gathered your sweaters, run them in the hot water cycle. Be sure to check on them every so often. All sweaters felt differently so you may need to run the load a few times. Then, throw them in the dryer.

When they are done, take that lint roller and clean out both your washer and dryer. (felting leaves a lot of lint behind!)

And now you have fabric to make anything you want out of! You can make stuffed animals, cushion covers, placemats...anything you can imagine. And you don't need a sewing machine either. If you decide to stitch something it's best to do it the old fashioned way...needle and thread. And if you've ever sewn a button on your pants, you can sew!

(Warning: once you start felting sweaters...you will be given more... people will start going through their closets to give you their old sweaters!)

Time

"You have exactly the same amount of hours in the day as Mother Theresa, Leonardo Da Vinci, & Albert Einstein."
-H Jackson Brown Jr.

"I don't have enough time."

This is by far the biggest excuse people use as to why they can't accomplish their goals. And I'm here to call total bullshit on this. This is why I have devoted an entire chapter to this topic.

We all have the same 24 hours in a day.

But why is it that some people manage to get more done than others?

Likely, they have learned to prioritize their actions, set healthy boundaries, and delegate the things they aren't good at. They know what builds momentum and what sabotages their energies. And, they spend the most time doing the most effective things to achieve their goals. Here are some of the main keys to good time management:

• Utilizing your strengths

• Asking for help

• Delegate tasks to other people while,

• Setting healthy boundaries

• Building your momentum and planning ahead for pitfalls

Utilizing Your Strengths

Here is the truth…You will never be *great* at something you have to work really hard just to be good at. Focusing too much energy on things other than your strengths will not only waste a lot of time but leave you feeling frustrated as well. But, if you put that time and energy into your natural talents, you will more quickly succeed. You should always utilize and cultivate your strengths. (Hint: your strengths are usually the things you feel confident doing.)

Having said that, some of our weaknesses do indeed need to be addressed before we can more effectively move forward in our lives. To successfully navigate those challenges, we require help.

Asking for Help

This is why therapists, coaches, trainers etc exist! People naturally want to help others. There is usually someone out there whom you can go to for help.

And for those of you who think asking for help is a sign of weakness, you're wrong. Ask any successful business owner if they did it all themselves and I assure you, they will say they had to get a LOT of help along the way.

So if you're stuck in some way…ask for help!

Delegate What You're Not Great At, and Set Strong Boundaries

Delegating tasks and setting boundaries can absolutely help you get more done. One of my most successful friends designs amazing film and television sets that have earned her 8 Emmy nominations. She's clearly pretty good at designing! But that's primarily all she focuses on...she doesn't paint, build or decorate the sets. She has excellent shoppers who are great at getting good deals. She has people working for her who are talented painters, carpenters, etc thus freeing up her time to stay focused on what she does best: designing.

She also is very clear about her boundaries. The prop master does not get to borrow from her art department, and visa versa. Having clear boundaries actually aids in keeping confusion to a minimum. With her crew, everybody knows where they stand which is why nobody's feelings get hurt when she says 'no'. (Go back and read 'Setting Healthy Boundaries' in chapter 4, 'Attitude Adjustment' if you skipped it!)

Build Momentum and Plan Ahead for Pitfalls

Another thing successful and motivated people do is take advantage of their momentum and avoid their pitfalls. They don't wait to take action...they just do it. Again, they are playing to their strengths so they already feel capable and confident. And, they are honest about their weaknesses when it comes to getting distracted or thrown off course. If social media is a threat, they don't go on Facebook on their lunch break. Instead, they may grab a cup of coffee or go for a walk. If they are trying to avoid sugar, they likely don't have candy in the house or at the office. If they know Netflix is addicting, they won't go near the TV until they are finished everything for the day. (Notice how many people write at Starbucks...likely they have too many distractions at home. They know they'll get more done if they are away from those temptations.)

This philosophy is now being utilized when patients are recovering from surgeries as well. They plan ahead for that moment they will want to bail on physical therapy, etc. That way when their resistance comes up, they are prepared and can more easily stick to their recovery plan. And, studies have shown that people who plan ahead to avoid their excuses, are more likely to have a faster and easier recovery.

The key then, once again, is to "know thyself" and honor your strengths and weaknesses.

So, when you look at your list of things to-do, ask: Do those actions play to your strengths? If not, who can help you get them done? What can you do RIGHT NOW to get the ball rolling and build some momentum? And where are you likely to slip up? (social media is the #1 time suck in my opinion...! Turn off those notifications!... unless you are actually utilizing social media to improve your business.) How can you take your distractions away? Are you agreeing to do too many things that kill your bliss?

Pick one of these strategies and implement it for the next week and see how much more time you can create for yourself.

Am I Running a Sprint or a Marathon?

If you are running a marathon, you run at a much different pace than a sprint. Usually, you run a marathon at a manageable, steady pace. It's a long, long run and you need to pace yourself to make it to the end.

A sprint is an all out burst of energy that it will only last a short time. If you ran a marathon at the speed of a sprint, you'd burn out before reaching the first mile.

You can use this question, sprint or marathon, for everyday life, and especially when stressful situations present themselves.

Asking myself this question, "Am I in a sprint or a marathon?" was key to me handling life when my father got cancer and suddenly passed away.

I was in a "sprint" in the beginning. I was dealing with doctors, hospitals, and home living logistics. And then funeral arrangements, financial adjustments, and notifications to credit companies, investments, etc.

But after that was finished, I entered the "marathon" of getting my mother's health and well-being taken care of. Without having her husband to rely on anymore, I had to pick up where he left off and make sure her needs were being attended to.

Sprints are "crunch time" moments. Pulling "an all nighter" and cramming for exams is a sprint. It's a pace you can keep up for a little while but will lead to destructive burnout if you function at that pace for too long.

Marathons are "long haul" projects. Going for your Ph.D. is a marathon. And you must pace yourself accordingly.

A screen test for a role in a film is the sprint. Filming on set for 6 months is the marathon.

Interviewing for several weeks for a higher position in the firm is a sprint.

Relocating and starting the new job is a marathon.

Asking yourself this question quickly informs you of the level of energy you will need to maintain for the next few days, weeks, months, or years. With this high level of clarity, you can tackle whatever challenge is ahead of you. And, you can be both effective and efficient without getting burned out.

Invoking Synchronicity

> *"Coincidence is God's way of remaining anonymous"*   - Albert Einstein

Synchronicity happens when you start taking bold steps towards following your passion. I've seen this countless times with every person I've ever worked with (including myself). The minute they step forward with courage and faith, the universe supports them in ways they could never have imagined. That old saying, "leap and the net will be there" is totally true. If you are acting in ways that support your greater good and the world as a whole, the universe will support your efforts three fold.

However, this doesn't happen while you're dreaming about your goals... it happens when you take deliberate, focused *actions* towards achieving them. I repeat: you must get off your butt and take deliberate, focused actions.

Resolving to lose the weight and hitting the road for a jog will likely have you noticing your local gym is running a sale for personal training. Deciding to finish the script by December 31st could attract an unexpected meeting with an agent interested in finding more clients. Committing to meditating every day for 30 days could cause your schedule to change in a way that makes it easier for you to sit and practice. Raising your rates could attract more high quality clients. (This happened for me. I raised my rates for new Pilates clients and got 3 new clients that week. They are amazing people and they are also paying at the new higher pay rate!) This is synchronicity at work.

But again, this kind of "luck" doesn't come from sitting at home doing nothing. It happens with action. You must move in the direction of your passion in order to receive the goodies of synchronicity.

Things to go back and Review:

- The 5 strategies for time management

- Sprint or Marathon

- Invoking Synchronicity

Kitty (or small dog) Teepee Craft

This is a DIY project I found at meowlifestyle.com She's got tons of other great projects on her site and is a huge cat fanatic...she also has tons of pictures of how to make her projects...definitely check her out if you enjoyed making this teepee.

You will need:

- 5 wooden dowels, or bamboo sticks, or twigs from your yard
- Scissors
- Scotch tape
- Hot glue gun
- Twine or leather chord
- Safety pins or needle and thread
- Towel or pillow or your repurposed sweater fabric for the bed
- Fabric for the teepee (this can be an old towel, scarf, or   anything you want to repurpose...but, if your cat is like mine, he might destroy his teepee every now and then, so choose a fabric you don't mind seeing clawed!)

Making the Teepee:

1.   Make 5 tape balls; pullout a bunch of tape and scrunch it up into a ball (not necessary if the teepee will be on carpet).

2.   Attach one to the bottom of each dowel (if they don't stay just glue them on).

3.   Gather 3 sticks. Hold them together at the top allowing the bottoms to flare out like a tripod (keeping one side wider for the entrance to the teepee).

4.   Wrap the twine around the gathered sticks (at the top).

5.   Apply a good amount of glue and continue to wrap a few more times.

6.   Add the 4th dowel and glue and wrap.

7.   Add the 5th dowel and continue to glue and wrap until the teepee can stand on it's own (I used a LOT of glue)

8.   Place your bed fabric in the teepee.

9.   Drape your teepee fabric over the teepee and safety pin it into place or stitch in place with needle and thread.

Warning...again, cats do like to thrash things...your teepee may be killed at times, but it can be resurrected quickly with another application of glue, and any new fabric you desire.

Final Thoughts and The Gift of Support

Here we are at the end...for now anyway. Remember that nothing in this book will help you if you don't actually DO the exercises. So, now is a perfect time to go back and try some of them out...if you haven't already.

Continue to do what you are passionate about. Try new things, express your creativity, and honor your individuality.

And most importantly know...nobody gets through this life alone. As I've said previously, we all need help sometimes.

GIVE YOURSELF THE GIFT OF SUPPORT

No addict ever got sober alone. No book was ever published without being edited by at least one other person. No house was built single handedly. No community was created in a bubble.

We *all* need support.

So look at your life, your goals, etc. Where are you struggling? Where could you use some extra support?

Go get it. *Now*. Be generous with yourself and get the support you need.

Book the therapy appointment. Buy a series of workouts with a trainer. Book your session with your health coach, writing coach, life coach, spiritual coach. Sign up now for that meditation class or painting class or college class.

As I said earlier, not having the money is no excuse. Sign yourself up *now*. The minute you step up by signing up, the funds show up. Remember, I've seen this more times than I can tell you. When you take a stand for yourself, the universe supports you...always.

And, by committing right away, you will feel both relieved and excited about your future.

Give this gift of support to yourself...*Now*.

You deserve it!

And, that includes reserving time with me! If that feels right to you, then get in touch and let's get a date on the books. My info is at the back of this book...and I'd love to hear from you.

Live with passion and joy. The world needs that special something that you were born to share. Please, don't wait. Start sharing your talents today.

xo

Brigitta

Additional Information:

Me!

> BrigittaDau.com
> brigittadaucoaching@gmail.com
> Collywobblecounty.com
> Collywobblecounty/etsy/shop.com

Sonesence Meditation tracks

My fave! Beautiful melodies and...she uses binaural beats... meditones...to replicate the theta brain waves we switch into when falling asleep. An amazing transformational tool. Follow my link bellow:

> *http://www.sonesence.com/shop/?ap_ id=Brigitta*

Big Huge Thank You's!!!!!

I have to thank my husband, Doug Warhit, first and foremost. He is my biggest cheerleader and best friend and I would not be the person I am today without his never ending love and support. I love you, baby!

Lindsey Smith-Sands was and still is an invaluable support for anything technical that needs doing. She is also a great friend, fellow crafter and a total nut, like me.

Collette Blonigan is responsible for all the great photography both in this book and on my etsy shop. She has a true talent for capturing people with their headshots. (And Collywobbles too!) Also an incredibly supportive friend...Thank you!

Jessica Cheney. Well, honestly, I wouldn't have this book or the crafts in it if it wasn't for our evolving friendship. Our friendship started while knitting together on our breaks while commiserating about how crappy our jobs felt. From there, with Jessica's support, my confidence flourished into not only becoming a full blown crafter...but becoming an etsy store owner and actually writing and selling patterns. And, you were my first 'goat yoga' accomplice! Babe, knowing you has changed my whole trajectory...for the better!

My entire knitting class and Wildfiber Studio! I must thank you all because you are such a supportive tribe...we joke about it being our therapy but I think it truly is. I've been able to show up in any shape or form always to feel safe and held by all of you. Plus you make me laugh my ass off every week!

Deanna Milligan, my soul sister...was a huge part of my support system when my Dad died. She encouraged my creativity and the notion to "just do what you love!"...and yes, the people (and the money) do indeed follow.

Tara Bliss, my life coach, has and still does have a huge impact on my life. I never would have taken the leap into life coaching let alone written a book, had it not been for her influence and support.

And a final thank you to all of my friends and clients (both Pilates and Life Coaching) for sharing your lives with me. I honestly love each and every one of you and would not be who I am today if it weren't for having you color my life with yours.

Made in the USA
Monee, IL
29 March 2025

14367532R00076